WIMBLEDON
2006

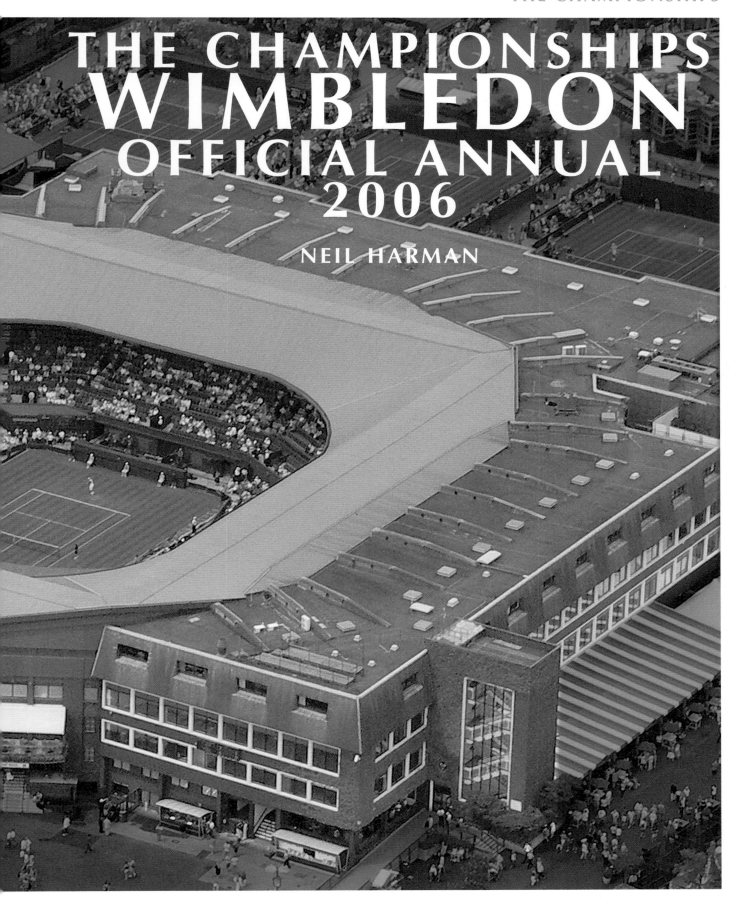

THE CHAMPIONSHIPS
WIMBLEDON
OFFICIAL ANNUAL
2006

NEIL HARMAN

Publisher
PPL Sport & Leisure

Managing Director
Bill Cotton

Art Editor
David Kelly

Design Team
Emma Robinson
Graham Nuttall
Caroline O'Donovan

Photography
Elaine Childs,
Getty Images UK

Editorial
Neil Harman

Editorial Liaison
Kevin McGoverin

Copyright (c) 2006
The All England Lawn Tennis
and Croquet Club

Photographs Copyright (c)
Getty Images

This first edition
published 2006 by
PPL Sport & Leisure
Century Building
Tower Street
Brunswick Business Park
Liverpool L3 4BJ

PPL Sport & Leisure
Bradford House
East Street
Epsom, Surrey KT17 1BL

PPL SPORT & LEISURE

ISBN 1-903381-16-9

Printed by Butler and Tanner

CONTENTS

FOREWORD
Tim Phillips

Chairman of The All England Lawn Tennis and Croquet Club
and Committee of Management of The Championships

The 120th Championships were a great success by any measure, with emotional farewells, exciting new faces and extraordinary tennis.

Wimbledon 2006 saw Andre Agassi and Martina Navratilova each playing their last match at Wimbledon. Andre, Wimbledon Champion in 1992, lost a wonderful match to Rafael Nadal, one of the new young lions of the game, and received adulations from a packed Centre Court. Martina Navratilova, the record nine times Wimbledon singles Champion, played her last doubles match some three months before her 50th birthday. Her retirement, after thirty Wimbledons, marks the passing of an era.

The top seeds won the men's singles and doubles and the ladies' singles. Roger Federer was majestic in retaining his title (his fourth in a row) for the loss of only one set. In a wonderful final he beat the world No.2 and French Open Champion, Rafael Nadal, in four memorable sets. This rivalry is taking men's tennis to sublime levels of skill and athleticism.

Amelie Mauresmo became our second ever French lady Champion and the first since Suzanne Lenglen in 1925. In the final she overcame any inhibitions, and Justine Henin-Hardenne, to record her first Wimbledon title – largely by going to the net unfashionably often.

Both our Champions are very popular figures and are great role models. We are proud to have them as our Wimbledon Champions 2006.

We enjoyed firsts in both the men's and ladies' doubles – Bob and Mike Bryan (World Champions) became the first identical twins to win the men's title and Zi Yan and Jie Zheng became our first Wimbledon Champions from the Peoples Republic of China – and surely not the last as tennis becomes increasingly popular there.

As always, Wimbledon generated drama and stories aplenty. I very much hope you will enjoy this story of the 120th Championships held at The All England Club. ●

INTRODUCTION
Neil Harman

As 50-week periods between Wimbledon Championships went, that which had separated the last exchange of 2005 from the first thunderbolt of 2006 had been tumultuous. For a start, a new chief executive, Ian Ritchie, a barrister, had been installed for 26-year stalwart Chris Gorringe; a new referee, Andrew Jarrett had taken the walkie-talkie and the rain-blame from Alan Mills and a new club secretary, Martin Guntrip stepped into the long-serving shoes of Roger Ambrose. Within three days of the end of the last year's event, London was awarded the 2012 Olympic Games and the tennis would be staged at the Club.

That was only the SW19 half of it. Roger Draper had replaced John Crowther as chief executive of the Lawn Tennis Association after nine years and British tennis awaited the effect of a new, self-confident broom. Etienne de Villiers had become the chairman and subsequently CEO of the ATP Tour replacing Mark Miles and a breath of freshness descended on men's tennis; there was upheaval at Tennis Australia with Peter Bellenger retiring as referee of the Australian Open, Steve Wood, a playing contemporary of former Wimbledon champion, Pat Cash, had taken over as chief executive and Paul McNamee stepped down as tournament director. Kim Clijsters, thankfully, had won a grand slam title for the first time at the US Open, so had Amelie Mauresmo, double thankfully, in Australia where a colourful Cypriot by the name of Marcos Baghdatis reached the men's final to mesmerising effect.

Rafael Nadal had beaten Roger Federer four times since February, all of them finals, the most recent of which had been to retain his French Open title.

New looks were everywhere. Even the umpires and the ice-cream at The Championships would be different in texture and taste. In March, a partnership had been announced with Ralph Lauren, the American designer, to become the official outfitter of Wimbledon until 2010.

Inspired by the tradition and English heritage of Wimbledon, the Ralph Lauren Collection would feature blazers, cardigans, jackets and polo shirts that would "make subtle use of the club colours and the cross rackets logo" to be sold internationally. There were a lot of extremely self conscious umpires on the first day.

And Haagen-Dazs had become the "Offical Wimbledon Ice-Cream" with themed outlets (what had become of the good old raspberry mivvi?) in the Aorangi Food Court and an ice cream parlour near to the food village. The Haagen-Dazs Cafe in Leicester Square would carry a Wimbledon theme throughout the fortnight. The Club had acquired a real sweet tooth.

Visiting the grounds a month before The Championships, to say that the place looked dishevelled was an understatement but as the event dawned, you would not have known that the hard-hats and digging equipment had only just been placed in cold storage for a fortnight.

Once The Championships were complete, the demolition and re-building of the existing Centre Court east side would begin, the reduction of the tea lawn levels commence, and the roof on Centre would be removed. Changes, changes, everywhere.

Amelie Mauresmo

And what about the Wimbledon Lawn Tennis Museum? HRH The Duke of Kent, President of the All England Club and Patron of the Museum had, on April 12, officially cut the ribbon on a building that would become a trend-setter of its type. Even the hoariest of critics could not help but marvel at the transformation. A far-too-lifelike ghost of John McEnroe escorted you around, recreating the Gentlemen's Dressing Room of the 1980s, relating, in his inimitable style, famous tales of yore.

Whatever you wanted, the museum could offer - an experience of what it was like to play on Centre Court in a remarkable 3-D cinema; watching interviews with the legends of the game; pitting one's power of speed, stamina and co-ordination in the *Reaction zone*; using interactive touch screens to bring to life the museum's extensive archive; through to the changing tennis fashions, from the heady days of Ted Tinling's designs to the contemporary styles of the Williams sisters, Maria Sharapova and the incomparable Rafael Nadal 'piratas'.

The All England Club was justly proud, too, of its Road to Wimbledon initiative, a junior programme that had enjoyed another successful year encouraging young people into the sport. At a national level, Tom Farqhuarson from Surrey (Farqhuarson Field by 2012 perhaps?) and Samantha Vickers (Lincolnshire) had had their names inscribed on the Club trophies after their respective victories in the Boys and Girls 2005

Road to Wimbledon National under-14 challenge.

In the local community, the WJTI (Wimbledon Junior Tennis Initiative) had allowed more than 37,5000 children from nearby state schools to learn the rudiments of, and be excited by, tennis, through the visit of an All England Club coaching team, the inspiration for which was Dan Bloxham.

All of these kids wanted to be Andy Murray - or the female equivalent - one day. The Centre Court was their aim, or so we justifiably hoped. A year on from his third round appearance there in 2005 that suggested so much to come, how was our hero? We met in Nottingham, three days before the championships. "A lot of people say that about me, that I'm permanently miserable on the court and in way, I agree," Andy Murray, offering the remnants of his prawn crisps, said. "I'd say to them - 'if you had to put up with everything I did when I was 18, how do you think you'd have felt?'"

One noted the use of the past tense - "when I was 18". Now that Murray was 19, were we about to witness the blooming of the boy from Dunblane? If he could translate the mood of our meeting into a permanent state of thoughtful good sense and mutual jousting, what a pleasure the next few years would be. "When my problems have been sorted out," he said, "I'll be the happiest guy on court."

Last year, entering Wimbledon he was a gangly thing ranked at No.312; he would start these Championships at No.45. In anyone's language, it was nothing short of meteoric and if he had stalled recently, with six wins from 18 matches since his breakthrough success on the ATP Tour, in San Jose in February, he was at pains to point out that he was on the course he set himself. The young man's talent could not be a factor, nor his willingness to embrace the illogical hopes pinned to a British tennis player of immense promise - especially in these two weeks.

"There have been difficult moments. I had to get something off my chest in Australia (blaming the press for putting too much pressure on him) and I think that did me good. I want to be myself and things get twisted. But I do think I'm beginning to understand what this is all about. Once my life gets sorted out, I won't have issues, I won't be getting down on myself and uptight. I think by the end of the year, you'll see a real change."

Indeed, change was the watchword of The 2006 Championships and as we hustled down Church Road on June 26, past the queues of people whose patience and forbearance we marvelled at, we wondered at what other changes we were about to bear witness. ●

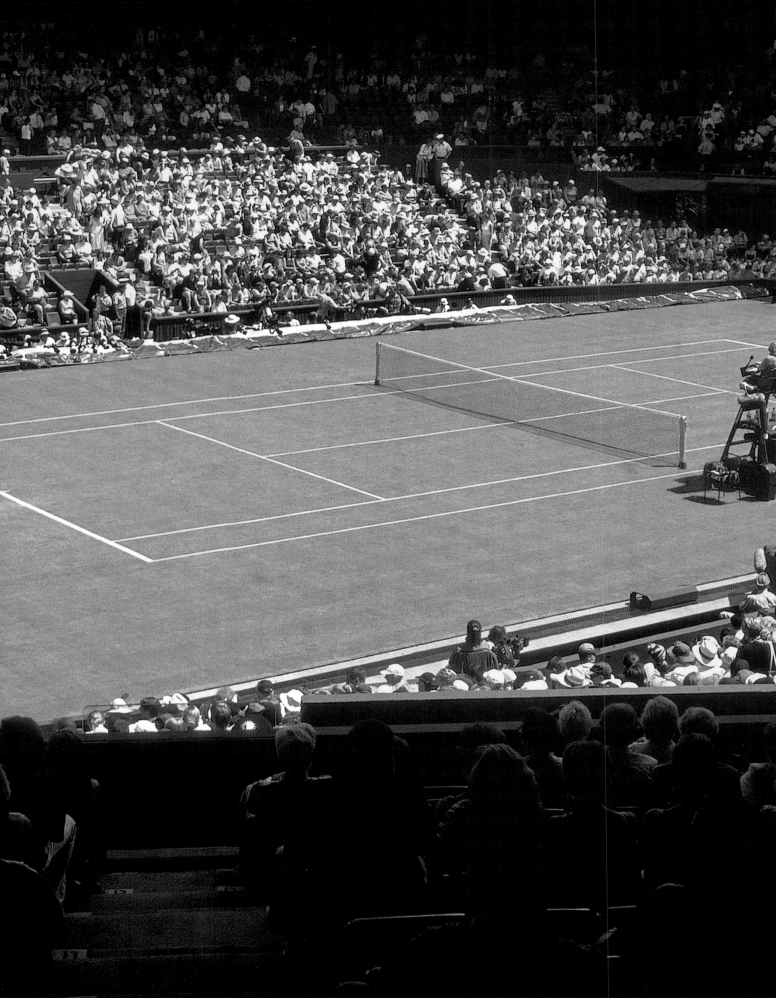

GAME, SET,
HISTORY.

 Wimbledon turns champions into legends. Since 1877, it has grown into the most coveted title in tennis; perhaps in all of sport. Its traditions, from the white dress code to the exact length requirement of the grass, are sacred. To play on Centre Court is the chance of a lifetime. To win, the chance to become a part of history. **THE WIMBLEDON CHAMPIONSHIPS – JUNE 26TH TO JULY 9TH, 2006.**

WWW.ROLEX.COM   OYSTER PERPETUAL DATEJUST

ROLEX

Roger Federer
Seeded 1st
Age: 24. Born: Basel, Switzerland.

Entered The Championships having equalled Bjorn Borg's record of 41 consecutive victories on grass in the Halle tournament. It is difficult to find the words to do his talent justice, the world No.1 reeks of splendour and calm assurance. Chasing a fourth consecutive Wimbledon title, he talked before of his "positive dreams" and strolled the grounds in the manner of a man on top of his game. He had won the US Open and Australian Open before losing in the final of the French Open to Rafael Nadal.

Rafael Nadal
Seeded 2nd
Age: 20. Born: Manacor, Majorca.

Had made no secret of the fact that, unlike many of his Spanish contemporaries and past players, he wanted to conquer the vagaries of grass. With a remarkable 60 consecutive victories on clay, including the retention of his Monte Carlo, Rome and French Open titles, Nadal carried all before him on one particular surface. A shoulder injury on the eve of the tournament unsettled his preparations but he could point to the fact that he had played Federer seven times and won six, four of those in finals in 2006.

Andy Roddick
Seeded 3rd

Age: 23. Born: Omaha, Nebraska, USA.

    Twice a beaten finalist at SW19, the tall, powerful American would not relent until the title he coveted, this one, was his to savour. Having come so close, having had the trophy snatched from him by Roger Federer in the past two years, Roddick had since dispensed with Dean Goldfine and was working with John, his brother. He had not had a particularly good year, reaching one semi-final (where he lost to Andy Murray in San Jose in February) and four quarter finals. On grass, though, he had beaten both Fernando Gonzalez and Nicolas Massu of Chile to help the US to the Davis Cup semi-finals.

David Nalbandian
Seeded 4th

Age: 24. Born: Cordoba, Argentina.

    The 2002 finalist had been a semi-finalist at each of the other three grand slams, but never been able take that last giant step again. Never really fancied his prospects on grass but the slower conditions offered him a great opportunity. He had finished in the top ten for the third year in succession, topping that off with an astonishing victory in the Tennis Masters Cup in Shanghai, having been called in as a late replacement. He had been planning on a fishing trip with his friends but instead he landed his biggest catch, beating Roger Federer in a memorable five set final.

Ivan Ljubicic
Seeded 5th
Age: 27. Born: Banja Luka, Bosnia-Herzegovina.

Ljubicic had a rare dislike of grass, which bordered on despair of his chances on the surface but this immensely likeable man had enjoyed the finest period of his career, reaching the Masters Cup in Shanghai and helping Croatia to their first Davis Cup victory which he regarded as astonishing for a refugee from the Bosnian town of Banja Luca who had been fostered by his Italian coach, Riccardo Piatti. He had finished in the top ten for the first time in his career.

Lleyton Hewitt
Seeded 6th
Age: 25. Born: Adelaide, Australia.

Since losing in the semi-finals of both last year's Wimbledon and the US Open to one and the same Roger Federer, Hewitt, the 2002 Champion, had contented himself with becoming a husband, marrying Bec Cartwright of *Home and Away* fame, and father to a daughter, Mia, born in November. His loss to Juan Ignacio Chela of Argentina in the second round of this year's Australian Open left a huge dent in proceedings and Hewitt then spent a period out to shake off ankle problems.

Returned to sparkling form in the French Open, carrying that over to win the Stella Artois title at Queen's Club for the fourth time.

Mario Ancic

Seeded 7th

Age: 22. Born: Split, Croatia.

Big serving, potent groundstroking Croatian who came into The Championships having won the Rosmalen tournament in Holland the previous week, underlining the belief of his compatriot, Goran Ivanisevic, that he was second favourite for the title behind Federer. Was the last man to beat the Swiss on grass, in the first round of 2002. Ancic had also had a distinctive clay court season, reaching the semi-finals of the Masters of Hamburg, and his first quarter final at Roland Garros.

James Blake

Seeded 8th

Age: 26. Born: Yonkers, New York, USA.

On the back of the finest year of his career, the American with a British mother, was now the second highest ranked from his nation behind Andy Roddick.

Had overcome manifold difficulties - not least the death of his father, Thomas, in 2004 - which caused him to suffer facial paralysis.

Played the match of 2005 against Andre Agassi at the US Open. This year, he'd won tournament titles in Sydney and Las Vegas and reached the final in Indian Wells, losing to Roger Federer and at Queen's where he was beaten by Lleyton Hewitt. Obviously, in the form of his life.

Amelie Mauresmo
Seeded 1st
Age: 27. Born: St Germain en Laye, France.

The consummate all-court player who had the game to win but always seemed to fall short, came significantly of age by winning the Sony Ericsson WTA Tour championships in Los Angeles in November and her first grand slam title, at the Australian Open when Justine Henin-Hardenne retired at 6-1, 2-0 down. It was not the way she might have wanted to win, but for Mauresmo, it was a huge breakthrough. She set off on a sequence of three further finals, in Paris, Doha and Antwerp, was beaten in the fourth round of her home grand slam by Nicole Vaidisova of the Czech Republic and, in Eastbourne, in her first match by compatriot, Nathalie Dechy.

Kim Clijsters
Seeded 2nd
Age: 23. Born: Bilzen, Belgium.

Had shocked the tennis world by announcing her intention to retire at the age of 25 to start a family, after which she promptly won the US Open for her first grand slam triumph after losing in four previous slam finals.

One of the nicest people in the sport, her victory in New York over Mary Pierce was warmly welcomed. Started 2006 ranked No.2 but was unable to reach a single final, being tripped up by constantly by her compatriot, Justine Henin-Hardenne, most recently in both the semi-finals of the French Open and Eastbourne.

Justine
Henin-Hardenne
Seeded 3rd

Age: 24. Born: Liege, Belgium.

Having been forced to miss The 2004 Championships through a viral illness and losing in the 2005 first round to Eleni Daniilidou of Greece, the Belgian waif still needed Wimbledon to complete her set of grand slam victories. Riding the crest of a wave, having won her second Roland Garros - beating Svetlana Kuznetsova in the final - the previous month and taking the Eastbourne title against Anastasia Myskina, most were expecting Henin-Hardenne to conquer. There would always be questions, though, about whether she was strong enough to keep going.

Maria Sharapova
Seeded 4th

Age:19. Born: Nyagan, Russia.

Sharpaova had been the Wimbledon junior runner up at 15, and the Champion at 17, so could she maintain her record of reaching a final at the All England every other year? A remarkable testament to her consistency was that Sharapova had, in her past 27 tournaments over 18 months, failed to reach the quarter finals only once and that was the French Open three weeks earlier, losing from a set up to Dinara Safina in the fourth round.

Svetlana Kuznetsova
Seeded 5th
Age: 20. Born: St Petersburg, Russia.

The 2004 US Open Champion who reached a career high No.4 in the world a month later, was not able to sparkle quite so spectacularly in 2005, though she kicked herself hardest for letting go of two match points in the fourth round to Justine Henin-Hardene. Her turnaround this year came at the Nasdaq-100 in Miami, in which she defeated Martina Hingis, Amelie Mauresmo and, in the final, Maria Sharapova. Then she reached the final of the French Open for the first time, losing to Henin-Hardenne, as was her wont.

Venus Williams
Seeded 6th
Age: 26. Born: Lynwood, California, USA.

The defending Champion, winning her fifth grand slam title as the No.14 seed, with an epic two hour, 45 minute final against Lindsay Davenport, the longest in Wimbledon history, Venus struggled with illness and injury during the latter half of the season, which she ended ranked No.10. Her start to 2006 was awful, a first round loss in the Australian Open to Tsvetana Pironkova, of Bulgaria, sent her into another spell on the sidelines, not returning to the circuit until April. Lost in the Rome semi-finals to Martina Hingis having won the first set 6-0 and fell to Nicola Vaidisova, of the Czech Republic, in the quarter final of the French.

Elena Dementieva

Seeded 7th

Age: 24. Born: Moscow, Russia.

    The finest hour for this tall, leggy blonde in 2005 had come at Roland Garros in the autumn where she inspired Russia to the retention of their Fed Cup title. She defeated both Mary Pierce and Amelie Mauresmo in singles, partnering Dinara Safina to the decisive doubles victory. Had a rude awakening in 2006, losing in the first round of the Australian Open to Julia Schruff of Germany, recovered to win the Japan Open in Tokyo and reach the final of Indian Wells, but lost to Shahar Peer, of Israel, in the third round of the French Open.

Patty Schnyder

Seeded 8th

Age: 27. Born: Basle, Switzerland.

    A consistent rather than dramatically gifted left hander, Schnyder could blow hot and cold in equal measure. In blistering conditions this year, she had reached the final of the Charleston tournament, as well as the semis, indoors, in Paris. In her previous ten appearances in SW19, she had reached the third round once and her previous best grand slam performance was reaching the semi-finals of the 2004 Australian Open.

    This year, in Melbourne, she had been beaten in the quarter finals by Amelie Mauresmo.

Day **ONE**
26.06.2006

Monday 26 June…

Only six full sets were completed on the first day of Andrew Jarrett's reign as Wimbledon referee, a perverse means of welcoming the former Derbyshire player into the seat vacated after 24 years by Alan Mills. At 7.20 pm came the announcement, with all the usual depressing undertones, that play had been called off for the day with not a single match completed and so many disappointed, rain-jacketed people scurrying for the exits.

The drizzle relented for 45 minutes, allowing Roger Federer to make an entry onto Centre Court that evoked memories of a distant era. No one could remember precisely when the last champion walked out in a tailored jacket, certainly not one with their surname and three rackets – signifying his three All England Club titles – embroidered on the breast pocket. It was a departure from convention that had the effect of making Federer stand out even more compellingly than usual.

Roger Federer

Asking around the press room as to who could recall the last time a man so resplendently attired had made his entry, the favourites were Donald Budge, Gottfried von Cramm, the German who lost in two finals to Fred Perry of Great Britain, and the flamboyant Bill Tilden of the United States. The wily veteran, Gianni Clerici of Italy's *La Repubblica* newspaper, said that though he was probably the worst player ever to compete in The Championships, in 1953, he walked on in a jacket that was now housed in the International Tennis Hall of Fame.

Far removed from the worst, Federer was being considered as one of the greatest ever. The 24 year-old Swiss had been pipped in the final of the French Open by Rafael Nadal, his attempt to become the sixth man in history to win all four of the grand slam tournaments scuppered by the boy wonder from Spain. On grass, however, the story was different, and the world no.1 had won the Gerry Weber Open in Halle, Germany, the habitual prelude to success on England's lawns. ➤

Richard Gasquet

Inasmuch as he had come close to being beaten a couple of times the week before The Championships, Federer still managed to equal Bjorn Borg's record of 41 grass court wins in succession, though he eschewed the thought that the All England Club might mark such an achievement with an on-court presentation as the French Federation had done when Nadal won his 53rd consecutive on clay on in Paris. They dragged Guillermo Vilas, the old record holder, out to hand Nadal a glass case full of bits of rock that purportedly represented the basic constituents of a clay court. Federer did not want a repeat performance. "I prefer presentations at the end of events, not during them," he said.

His initial burst against Richard Gasquet, of France, suggested his thoughts may have turned already to a few days hence. He started, and ended, the first set with an ace and it was 26 minutes of the most divine tennis. Gasquet, winner of the grass-court title in Nottingham two days earlier and possessed of a potent game of his own, lost his first serve to a beguiling Swiss mix of backhand slices and popped forehand winners.

Rain delay

Gasquet, too, is a throwback to days when a tennis racket was more rapier than blunderbuss. There is a distinct swish through the air, he takes a full cut at his groundstrokes, and his backhand is a thing of real beauty. Chances against Federer on grass are few and far between and when the 20 year-old had one chance, to have taken a break point in the fifth game, his decision to go down the line when close to the net was brilliantly intercepted by the Swiss for a winning forehand volley. They were chased from the court with Federer leading 6-3, 1-2, a significant lead but nothing more.

Elsewhere, matches had begun but it was a thoroughly awful way to spend the first Monday of a grand slam championship, looking for odds and ends. So, it was time to catch up with a few *bon mots* from John McEnroe, three times a Champion at the All England Club, which, when he defeated Bjorn Borg in 1981, refused him the customary automatic membership because of his 'poor behaviour and antics'.

McEnroe, ever the character, said: "That didn't feel that bad, to be honest. In fact, I felt good about it. Why would I want to be a member of a club that treated me that way, that didn't get me and I didn't get them?

"The irony is that it seemed back then like the inmates were running the asylum: myself, (Jimmy) Connors, (Ilie) Nastase earlier, and some of the other players. Then they tightened the rules too much, I believe. They stifled personality as if they wanted some communist system where there were just robots out there. And I think they realised over time that that's not a good thing. Now tennis is becoming more like well, I don't want to say, a niche sport. But when I first went to London there were three TV stations, now you have hundreds. You have to fight for an audience. You have to sell your personalities."

Conversation shifted the the great British dilemma over Tim Henman, McEnroe suggesting it was "regrettable" that so many see as failure a career that took him to four Wimbledon semi-finals. "England's attitude has changed. You are not so accepting of good losers, you no longer believe that the main thing is maintaining your manners." But wasn't it McEnroe, disputing line calls as if world peace hung on them, who changed us for the worse?   ➢

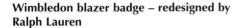

Wimbledon blazer badge – redesigned by Ralph Lauren

"I agree that the way America viewed it was too much the other side; win at all costs, almost. But the Wimbledon final I lost to Bjorn (in 1980) was the most talked-about match of my career. It elevated me in respect among the players, fans, even the media. It is a good lesson to tell my kids; you don't necessarily have to win them all."

We peered outside and the rain was still trickling down, the covers across all courts, the scenario not good. It was a day to have a peek at the new Museum, a grand structure, where Tim Phillips, the club chairman, had accompanied both Federer and Maria Sharapova, to their delight. Yelena, Maria's mother, had returned to

Russia the day before The Championships, having spent a week picking up after, and chilling out with, her daughter, striking a perfect balance of relaxation and routine before the 19 year-old set out on yet another Wimbledon episode.

The Museum experience was not to be missed. "You usually go to museums to see marvellous paintings and stuff but to see myself there, to be considered part of the history of this Championship, the way they have made it come to life, was amazing," Sharapova said. "We, as players, often say how much Wimbledon is the centre of tennis for us and now the fans, through

the exhibits, can see the whole story and it makes it so real for everyone."

It is four years since Sharapova had first walked through the gates to play the junior championship – she lost in the final to Vera Douchevina, her fellow Russian – two more since she turned the sport on its axis by defeating Serena Williams, the defending Champion, to win the title. It remained her only grand slam tournament victory, setting a course for a lifetime's mix of sporting endeavour and paparazzi clamour. At least, this year, the cameras have moved from outside her front door to outside any restaurant in Baden-Baden where the wives and girlfriends of England's World Cup footballers had convened.

Sharapova felt contented and liberated. Those who pointed to the interfering demands of outside activities would do well to consider that, of her past 27 tournaments over 18 months, Sharapova had failed to reach the quarter finals only once and that was the French Open three weeks earlier, losing from a set up to Dinara Safina in the fourth round. In Paris, though, she was struggling on her injured foot, whereas the grass has offered her the chance to move more freely and unleash her full repertoire.

And she is a long way from the finished article. ➢

"We go about our lives and don't think about age," she said, "It is as if we should be adults. Normal 19 year-olds don't spend over ten months a year travelling the world in such a competitive environment with all the attention, all the expectations that come with the package. I go with the flow – with what has to be done. If you don't like it, you can go home and watch the tournament on TV but, unfortunately, you won't have a chance to win. And that's why I'm here.

"This is the beginning of my career, I still have a lot of improving to do in order to be at the peak of my game and as long as I still have that feeling…because I love this. It is the reason I am training as hard as I can, to be there on Saturday, playing for that plate. I've been there, I've felt it and you want it so much more.

All the work and dedication makes those feelings worthwhile."

We awaited her entrance with bated breath. ●

Day **TWO**
27.06.2006

HENMAN
vs
SODERLING

RUSEDSKI
vs
SAFIN

AGASSI
vs
PASHANSKI

WAWRINKA
vs
KARLOVIC

DELGADO
vs
BERRER

BLOOMFIELD
v
BERLOCQ

MURRAY
v
MASSU

RODDICK
v
TIPSAREVIC

Andy Murray

Janko Tipsarevic

Tuesday 27 June…

The clouds had scattered, the artifical sprinklers were back in operation replacing the real deal from the skies above and from the remnants of a desperately disappointing Monday came a Championships' schedule enough to whet the most voracious appetite.

To compensate for the mishaps on Day One, four matches, rather than the usual three, were scheduled on both the prime show courts, with Andy Murray returning to the scene of his grand slam birth in the last match on Centre Court and beating Nicolas Massu 6-1, 6-4, 6-4 and Andy Roddick, twice a runner-up, scheduled to complete the programme on No.1 against the feisty Serb with the metal studs in his right eyebrow, Janko Tipsarevic, Roddick winning 6-7, 6-4, 7-6,6-2.

That, of course, required the matches ahead to be completed without undue delay and Tim Henman, now Britain's No.3, wrapping up his meeting with Robin Soderling of Sweden as quickly as possible.

Tim winning easy? Do us a favour. Henman and No.1 Court have never been the most comfortable of bedfellows – for some reason he has found it difficult to do domination on a court where players often struggled for spectator intimacy.

Soderling had reached the semi-finals of the Red Letter Days Open in Nottingham the previous Friday and could be expected to offer stiff resistance. Even the Swedes were not exactly sure how to take him; he wasn't one of the chummier ones, like Jonas Bjorkman or Thomas Johansson, he was steely eyed, crew-cutted and square-jawed. Henman clawed his way through the match 6-7, 6-3, 6-2, 1-6, 6-3, describing the it as "pretty routine as five setters go." He had to be kidding.

The British contingent in the men's draw was reduced by a significant one as Greg Rusedski, the No.1 player from the home shores entering the tournament, was beaten in straight sets, 6-4, 6-4, 6-4, by Marat Safin of Russia, who had spoken on the eve of The Championships of his renewed

focus and determination not to spend the last four years of his career – he had given himself that amount of time – ranked in the 60s or 70s. The top ten was his aim once more and with his new seriously cropped hair (thank goodness, the hideous Parisian ponytail had hit the barber's shop floor!), you had to take him seriously.

Rusedski was a disappointment but said he was struggling throughout with a recurrence of the hip problem that had dogged him since Roland Garros. "I've had more comebacks than most players, bar Mr Agassi perhaps," Rusedski said. "You need to see how much you have left in the tank and whether you really want to come back." ➤

Andy Murray

As for Mr Agassi, the look on his face was of a reprieved, resuscitated man. Andre Agassi had appeared on Centre Court to one of those ovations that causes the hardest of hearts to soften. They stood and cheered him to the chair, they applauded as he unwrapped his rackets and he had to blow them kisses *before* the coin-toss before they stopped applauding.

As he had only been their Champion once, 14 years ago, Agassi's reception from a predominantly British crowd may have taken even him by surprise. But by announcing his intention to retire from competition when he loses in the US Open later this summer, the 36-year-old American sucked the sting from those who, on the evidence of the first and fourth sets yesterday, might have openly questioned why he carried on at all. Therefore, each loving decibel was very much his proper due. But it fazed Agassi more than he had expected.

He was nervous, unsure, worried. His hands were trembling. "I just wanted to do 'em proud," he said.

Thank goodness the match worked out as it did, for how could he have possibly dealt with defeat to a part-Serb, part-Maltese who had not played in the main draw of Wimbledon in his life? Thus, Agassi's 2-6, 6-2, 6-4, 6-3 victory over an increasingly rattled Boris Pashanski, who has reached No.69 in the world ranking largely by virtue of his success on clay, was greeted much as if our hero had escaped without injury from a car wreck.

For the first 32 minutes, by which time he was a set down and growling inside, Agassi's return to Wimbledon, after a three year absence, did have the smell of an accident waiting to happen. It is not often that aces are required to keep him in games, but Pashanski had not had to play too far above himself to look like a competent challenger – Agassi's movement was badly restricted, especially if he was forced to move wide to retrieve.

Steffi, his wife, looked a lost soul, sitting in the member's enclosure with an empty seat on either side of her; Darren Cahill, his coach, was ➤

Andre Agassi

similarly in splendid isolation in the players' box.

Agassi looked similarly alone. Something was needed to perk him up and it came when Pashanski, who may have suddenly realised where he was, and who he was playing, missed a backhand service return that would have given him a 2-0 lead in the second set. He was broken for the first time in the next game, appealing in vain that Agassi's groundstroke, that forced him

to balloon his forehand long, had landed long.

Agassi began to settle more into his groove, Pashanski was happy to feed him on the diet of mid-court balls at which he was able to open his shoulders and, if nowhere near vintage, his victory was as sweet as any he has managed in recent times. Having missed The 2004 Championships with a hip injury, and last year to the effects of the sciatic nerve problem that has

MATCH of the Day

ROGER FEDERER
VS
RICHARD GASQUET

Roger Federer beat Richard Gasquet 6-3, 6-2, 6-2. A real Champion's opener. When the draw was made, it appeared as if this was the toughest route a defending Champion had to the second week since Pete Sampras mine-infested route in 1996, when he lost in the quarter finals to Richard Krajicek. First up for the Fedmeister was Gasquet, the supremely talented Frenchman, who had defeated the Swiss in Monte Carlo in 2005 but Federer was more than equal to the challenge. His movement was wonderful, his touch secure and long before the end, he had drained the 20 year-old's reserves of confidence, so that Gasquet – one of the real talents in the world – was reduced to slapping wildly at the ball.

Champion, into painful submission. Karlovic was the runner up at the Stella Artois Championship at Queen's Club last year; this year he had forgotten to enter the tournament, and lost in the first round of qualifying, so he was obviously not the clearest of thinkers.

Give him a ball in his hands, though, and he is a terrifying prospect but Wawrinka did himself proud as well as cheering up an awful lot of other players in his section of the draw, by defeating Karlovic 7-6, 3-6, 6-2, 6-7, 11-9. From the long, the tall, to the short.

Jamie Delgado had been a fixture on the British tennis map longer than most of those still wielding a racket and though he was into the draw, it was still not enough for him to be figured in the official LTA media guide to British participants. An unfortunate oversight, made more so by the fact he would win a pulsating five set match against Michael Berrer, a German who had been seeded No.5 in the qualifying. ➤

hastened his retirement, Agassi just wants to swing free and feel the grass beneath his feet for one last, competitive time.

Stanislas Wawrinka of Switzerland – who had beaten Andy Murray in a Davis Cup tie in Geneva in 2005 – had looked the most morose man in SW19 when he was paired in the opening round with Ivo Karlovic, the 6'10" Croatian who, in 2003, had clubbed Lleyton Hewitt, the defending

Delgado had earned his place in the main draw by winning the LTA's wild card play off and his victory meant he had reached the second round for the third time in nine attempts. He represented, in pure tennis terms, a tremendous athlete, possessed of a backhand that most players could only dream off. Something, though, had stopped him progressing as he ought and the argument about his comparative lack of inches should not have mattered – look at the Rochus brothers from Belgium, even Andre Agassi. They were hardly leviathans.

"My body is feeling better than it was a couple of years ago," Delgado said. "If I stay fit and healthy and working on the right things., I still feel I have enough years ahead where I can achieve a lot in the game. I'm as excited as I have ever been."

Richard Bloomfield's rise up the rankings – he would reach a career high No.200 the week after The Championships – was extremely noteworthy. The Norfolk totem was one of those players who, you felt, ought to have made more of an impact, given he stood over 6' tall and could boom his

serves down. His misfortune in the past two Wimbledons, had been to draw players of the renown of Feliciano Lopez of Spain and Antony Dupuis, the Frenchman.

This time, he was playing Carlos Berlocq, an Argentine, who had never set foot on a grass court before. Whether it was this, or that Berlocq had apparently picked up an ankle injury during the recent French Open, it sparked an enormous run of money on Bloomfield to win that provoked Betfair, the internet company, to contact the International Tennis Federation and let them know of their suspicions.

Poor Bloomfield knew nothing about this until he was asked, after a convincing 6-1, 6-2, 6-2 victory, whether he had ever been tempted to put a bet on himself. "Definitely not, I'm not that kind of person," he said. "I've hardly had a bet in my life, I don't know how to play poker. I'm not into that kind of stuff." Did he mind being labelled as a brave Brit? "A little bit," he replied. "We all try to do our best. Maybe that is 150 in the world. But we are trying to get up there. We all work hard." ●

Day **THREE**
28.06.2006

VERDASCO
VS
BECKER

WILLIAMS
VS
MATTEK

MAURESMO
VS
ABRAMOVIC

HINGIS
VS
GARBIN

KUZNETSOVA
VS
PESCHKE

FEDERER
VS
HENMAN

LJUBICIC
VS
LOPEZ

LEE
VS
NORMAN

Bethanie Mattek

Wednesday June 28...

At 9.38 pm on Court 19, Fernando Verdasco of Spain raised an arm in triumph having beaten B. Becker to reach the third round of Wimbledon for the first time in a match watched, during daylight time, by B. Becker from the roof of the Broadcast Centre. Confused?

Well, Boris Becker – the three time Champion – had flown in from Germany for a couple of days rest from his TV duties at the FIFA World Cup, just in time to see Benjamin (no relation), who had survived the rigours of qualifying, attempt to reach somewhere he had never been before, the final 32 of a grand slam. The match went on and on and on. The office lights from the LTA Enclosure on the adjacent Court No.1 lent the atmosphere an eerie tone.

Elsewhere in the grounds, most players had gone home, their matches stopped at appropriate junctures at the end of sets, but Becker and Verdasco hung so precariously in the balance, there was no way – until total darkness fell – that it could be halted. Eventually, after 315 points, very few of which came easily, Verdasco

triumphed 6-4, 6-7, 4-6, 6-3, 9-7 and a third day of tumultuous happenings had come to an end.

It had seemed an age earlier when, on the first match on Centre Court, a girl from Minnesota – where it does get exceedingly chilly – by the name of Bethanie Mattek had strode onto court alongside that paragon of all things fashionable, Venus Williams. The entry of the ladies defending Champion, normally at 1 pm prompt on Tuesday, had been delayed by the miserable weather of Monday but it was well worth waiting for.

The tournament had already seen a dress by Stella McCartney and an outfit shot through with petal perforations worn by the beautiful Maria Sharapova. Out-dazzling them all – for presumptuousness as much as anything else – Miss Mattek wore knee length socks, which she had matched with tiny white shorts, the kind that 1970's kids wore. Above these was a singlet, resplendent with the logos for a chocolate firm and an online travel advisory service. After she had been thrashed 6-0, 6-1 for her reverse of 15 minutes of fame – the match lasted 51 minutes – answers were demanded.

Miss Mattek was watching the World Cup on

Venus Williams

42

TV when she learned of the order of play so she wanted to make a soccer statement. She walked to Harrods and spent a tenner on the socks, the shorts she had found in Paris after her first round defeat at Roland Garros. The top she was handed just before walking onto court, because for the lower ranked players – Mattek was No.103 in the Sony Ericsson WTA order – advertising agencies offer deals according to which court a player appears on. Centre = Big Bucks.

Mattek was paid $1,000 for each patch. "Without fans or support, or sponsors, I'd just be hitting a ball for my own entertainment," Mattek said. At the US Open last year, she was fined for walking onto court wearing a cowboy hat. She has also appeared in leopard-print dresses.

Had she heard of Gussie Moran, who caused a scandal at Wimbledon wearing lace-trimmed knickers, designed by the legendary Teddy Tinling, in 1949? "I want a picture of that, that's cool, I'll do it next year," she said. We awaited her return with interest.

Williams strode on, as did Sharapova, as had Amelie Mauresmo, beating Ivana Abramovic of Croatia 6-0, 6-0 in 39 minutes. Gerry Armstrong, the umpire, was not the first to be grateful to be paid on a daily rather than an hourly rate. Martina Hingis had not fussed at being asked to start her match as the evening shadows lengthened as she defeated Tathiana Garbin for the loss of three games. Only Svetlana Kuznetsova of the ➤

Martina Hingis after beating Tathiana Garbin

Roger Federer

Tim Henman against Federer.
Staring defeat in the face

grand slam champions in the field had shown a degree of compassion, defeating Kveta Peschke of the Czech Republic 6-4 in the third set.

Compassion? Roger Federer is a multi-linguist and doesn't usually lose much in any translation but one word tripped him up yesterday. He was asked if he felt compassion for Tim Henman and once it was was explained to him, his answer was that he did not. This is a brutal sport and Henman had just been brutalised by the radiance of the Wimbledon Champion.

In an hour and 25 minutes on Centre Court yesterday, the finest British grass court exponent of three generations was stripped bare by the world No.1. Not the great Pete Sampras, not Goran Ivanisevic, not Lleyton Hewitt, not even Dmitry Tursunov, have humbled Henman as he was humbled on the court of his dreams in front of a crowd that didn't know if it should laugh with Federer or cry for him. It was as if the Tiger had been taken to the taxidermists.

The end of Wimbledon for Henman came at

QUOTE of the Day

"I was able to be close to him when I was 17, 18, walking through the hallways. He knows every doorman's name, and please and thank yous at the transportation area. Those things don't get reported on, but they make the man more so than anybody. If I think dropping to No.5 is bad, I think about him dropping to No.141 and making it back to No.1 in the world. He was the ultimate guy at proving people wrong when they stuck a fork in him."

ANDY RODDICK ON THE
RETIREMENT OF ANDRE AGASSI

the same second round stage as last year when Tursunov, the Russian, culled him in five sets.

Yesterday, it was three, one competitive, one utterly one-sided and the last which might have been just as one-sided had the Swiss not been lured into a couple of mishits that prompted John McEnroe to suspect he didn't want to beat Henman love and love in consecutive sets. Which goes to show that McEnroe doesn't know as much about the man as he thinks he does.

Federer did not want to offer up the slightest hope, either to a player ranked No.64 or anyone else watching the match through their fingers, that he might accommodate pity. He can probably remember 1999 when he lost 6-0 sets in three successive matches, to Vince Spadea in Monte Carlo, Pat Rafter at the French Open and Byron Black, of Zimbabwe, at Queen's. They hurt like hell. But you just have to keep going.

Henman will do just that, which is to everyone's benefit in British tennis not least Andy Murray who doesn't need the crown of promise ➤

Ivan Ljubicic

to be placed on his head and be left in splendid isolation just yet.

Henman has never been less than the consummate professional and until the first ball is struck he will continue to go into any match – so long as he is not hurting physically – believing in his ability to win.

In the company of those he trusts, he will take stock of what a 6-4, 6-0, 6-2 defeat tells about whether he can compete at the levels he requires to be completely satisfied. He says there are a lot of challenges he wants to embrace, that he has been hitting the ball well and feeling stronger which bodes optimism. And he insisted at the outset of 2006 that he would make a mature judgement at Christmas about how long his career would be extended.

Spending the last ten days of Wimbledon at home with his daughters, while blissful in one respect, is a eye-opener in another. Bouncing the girls on his knee is not the same as bouncing a tennis ball on the grass but it does offer time to clear one's head and make the judgements that are imperative. He cannot beat Federer – very few can – and that is what it will take to win this Championship – indeed, his last title was at the BNP Paribas Masters in Paris, in November 2003 and two-and-a-half years without lifting a cup is an eternity for someone of Henman's class.

Despite his huge serve and all-court instincts, Ivan Ljubicic had rarely been happy with his performances at Wimbledon. In six previous appearances, he had never made it past the second round. But this distinctive man had improved in the past year; leading Croatia to its first Davis Cup win and soaring as high as No.3 in the rankings behind Federer and Rafael Nadal. He still did not relish grass but maintained an even strain throughout the marathon fifth set against Feliciano Lopez, a quarter finalist in 2005. Ljubicic rallied from an early break and kept applying pressure with his returns as Lopez continued to save match points, finally winning 6-3, 6-4, 5-7, 3-6, 11-9 when the Spaniard dumped his last left-handed serve into the net for a double fault.

In all, the match lasted four hours and three minutes; a long run for a grass-court match in which so many of the points seemed to be extremely short. Such encounters – full of big serves and acrobatic volleys – used to be the staple of Wimbledon but they are now almost as exotic as Australians in the main draw, the numbers of which were at their lowest in the Open Era.

"It's a fantastic win for me," said Ljubicic, who was out on Court 13 long enough to lose track of the number of match points Lopez saved. ➤

Martin Lee

To make it past the second round for the first time, Ljubicic will have to beat another serve-and-volley player with a yen for grass: the less graceful but more enthusiastic Justin Gimelstob of the United States. "Of course, I have had many years to think about why it's not good; it should be good," said Ljubicic of his grass-court game.

"On clay, I play similar to hard," he added. "On grass, you have to change. Today, I played more serve-and-volley than any time in my life. You just have to. Otherwise, the other guy will come to the net, and you don't want that. You have to make

adjustments, and I think I was not flexible enough in the past to really commit myself to changing."

Martin Lee, from Kent, was playing Dick Norman, from Belgium, the second oldest man in the field, on Court No. 10 and had reached a third set tie-break. From their perch on Court No.3, the BBC's Jonathan Overend and Mark Petchey strained their necks to report on it, the first recorded commentary of any match on this outside of all outside courts. Lee's performance was worthy of such history, a 6-2, 7-6, 7-6 success that pleased Millwall supporters everywhere. ●

SHOCKS of the Day

MELANIE SOUTH (GB) *beat* FRANCESCA SCHIAVONE (Italy) *3-6, 6-3, 6-3;* SARAH BORWELL (GB) *bt* MARTA DOMACHOWSKA (Pol) *6-3, 6-7, 6-4.* Two of the five British wild cards in the women's draw, they did not have the easiest of first round matches, especially South, who was facing the Italian 11th seed. A member of the Wimbledon Club across the road, for whom she plays National Club League "they have lovely grass courts there as well" she said, South transferred some fine form against a player who fancied her opportunities on grass. From No.305 in the rankings, she now had set her heart on the top 100. At 26, Borwell, from Middlesbrough, could be described as a late bloomer and boy what a blooming against Domachowska. A lot of it was put down to her love of Yugoslav music "I listen to it before I go on court," she said. "Everyone else thinks it's horrendous, but it pumps me up."

Day **FOUR**
29.06.2006

NADAL
VS
KENDRICK

WILLIAMS
VS
RAYMOND

MURRAY
VS
BENNETEAU

RODDICK
VS
MAYER

Venus Williams

Thursday June 29…

There are many days in the first week of Wimbledon when you feel you are in permanent pursuit of your tail. Turn your back for a moment and you are liable to receive a nasty surprise.

Sitting on the Centre Court on Wednesday, watching Roger Federer dismantle Tim Henman, a score flashed up from an outside court that told of a magnificent achievement by Melanie South, from Great Britain, in her first Wimbledon, who had beaten Francesca Schiavone, the 11th seed from Italy. What was *that*?

The same thing occurred on Thursday when the centre of attention was Rafael Nadal in glorious duel with Robert Kendrick, a graduate of Pepperdine University in Seattle, whose childhood appeared to have been idyllic, as he talked later of time spent in places like Sanibel Island, Fresno and Copper River. But I digress.

While Nadal was having his hands full of Mr Kendrick, and was giving the Centre Court crowd a demonstration of the wiles, the brute force and the never-say-die attitude that has served him so marvellously on the red clay, across the way on Court No.1, Venus Williams, the defending Champion, was a set and 5-2 down to Lisa Raymond, her fellow American. Pause for sharp intake of breath and re-focusing of attention. ➤

Lisa Raymond

Raphael Nadal

Robert Kendrick

Though Williams had lost to Raymond in a grand slam before, in the third round of the 2004 Australian Open, to see her treated with such indignity on grass was a real shock. A look into her eyes, though, was enough to indicate that she was not going to let the matter rest.

Despite the fact that Raymond was hitting the ball with tremendous cleanliness, going for her shots, Venus was not for beating.

Normal service – as well as normal backhands and forehands – was resumed as Venus began to nail the lines and Raymond could not quite sustain her early levels. Williams won 6-7, 7-5, 6-2. "I just picked up my techniques and it was a matter of me getting one game (when she trailed 5-2)," Venus said. "I just seemed to get another break and another break. It was all very exciting because I was happy that that third set was a lot smoother than the first two. But give her credit for putting me into a position when I really had to fight for it."

The same was definitely true of Nadal. Say what you will about the guy, but it is impossible

to take your eyes from him. The expectation was that Kendrick, ranked No.237 and a successful qualifier, would be rolled over in next to no time. This was his first grand slam appearance on a show court, and they do not come any more intimidating. And Kendrick arrived with an utterly refreshing attitude, that he would go for Nadal from the off, attack being the finest form of defence.

It proved to be a compelling tussle – it looked ominous for Nadal when Kendrick's cocktail of thumping serves, intuitive volleys and booming ground strokes secured him a two set lead. But British fans, as yet unexposed to Nadal's insatiable desire, were to glean exactly what makes the man as formidable as a Majorcan mountain.

Even then, it required an infinitesimal drop in Kendrick's exemplary level before Nadal could impose himself. Then, he was within two points of losing his place in the draw. But as Andre Agassi, who would face the winner, noted wryly at the time: "He (Kendrick) has to get over the finish line which is probably still a mile away."

It was not for the want of trying. At 5-4 and ➤

30-all in the fourth, Kendrick may have thought he had reached match point when a forehand drive from Nadal seemed to elude the baseline. Kendrick appealed; the crowd jeered, even Nadal looked sheepish, but television replays would prove Cedric Mourier, the French Open men's final umpire, correct and from there, Nadal never looked back.

Nadal won 6-7, 3-6, 7-6, 7-5, 6-4 in 18 minutes short of four hours.

It was a five set match in the very best traditions of five set matches, not a single one of them one sided. They contained all the magic ingredients one has learned to expect from matches involving this remarkable Spaniard. That, and the growing feeling that he was being persecuted from all sides, for delaying time between points, for choosing three balls on every serve – even when they were new, or there had been a 'let – for what would be termed general prevarication.

"I don't know what's happening in the past months, with the referees (umpires)," he said. "It's strange because they are putting a lot of pressure on me all the time. Today, he gave me a warning for time when I am putting the ball for a serve. After Rome, when Federer said I had coaching, and when Ljubicic say time at Roland Garros, I don't know if it's for that reason, no? But maybe the referees need to look more, because it is not my fault sometimes. So that's not nice for me."

It was not that nice to be in Andy Murray's position when the curtain was drawn on the Fourth Day. Brits had been falling all around him, Martin Lee had lost to Jarkko Nieminen of Finland in straight sets, Jamie Delgado had given Sebastien Grosjean a pretty decent run for his second round winners' money before losing in four; Melanie South and Sarah Borwell had fallen by the wayside, so Murray was the man.

Well, he was two thirds the man.

The 19 year-old was on the verge of completing the Saturday extravaganza that the All England Club had been praying for since the men's singles draw was made – Andre Agassi v. Rafael Nadal and Andy Roddick v. Scotland the Brave – when he took his eye off the main chance and was forced to trudge off Centre Court knowing he would return the following day with at least one further set to play.

Murray, the British No.2, had led Julien Benneteau of Bourg-en-Bresse, France (chicken farming country, I'm led to believe) by two sets and 4-2. It would have been rather presumptuous to suggest he started to see Roddick's serves in his mind's eye because Benneteau had proved throughout to be an intrepid competitor, one who matched the Scot audacious shot for audacious shot, drop shot for drop shot, tumble for tumble, brilliant winner for brilliant winner, gesture for gesture.

Maybe it is well that the light had begun to fade in concert with Murray's late third set form, because if he had been made to continue, the likelihood is that we would have been contemplating a one set shoot-out sometime later the following afternoon. That would not have been good for anyone with a suspect circulation. The first game offered an inkling of the labours to come. Murray had to save a couple of break points, the first with an ace, the second when he tempted Benneteau to strike a running forehand a touch wide. The trend of nip and tuck had been set. So had the course of the match which would become a mixture of confusing waves and eddies.

At the intermission, Murray leads 7-6, 6-4, 4-6 but it was Benneteau, a curly haired, slim, gutsy competitor, who had a subtle psychological advantage. There were a couple of teeth-grinding moments when Murray, who has never been the steadiest on his feet, tumbled over, clutching first the black protector on his left ankle, and then his right as he endeavoured to turn around a 3-0 deficit in the second set after he had taken the first in a thrilling tie-break. That set had seen the first in a series of drop shots that were so poorly executed that only someone not possessed of the Scot's doggedness would have dropped the tactic forthwith.

Left: Julien Benneteau

Right: Andy Murray – 'never been the steadiest on his feet'.

Andy Roddick

SHOCK of the Day

RAFAEL NADAL v. ROBERT KENDRICK.

Not only that the French Open champion was within two points of losing in the second round to a qualifier with a ranking of 237, who he had no information on "what you know about Kendrick?" he asked as we passed each other in the restaurant, but that when a linesman collapsed from what appeared to be exhaustion and it took so long for first aid to come to his assistance. "A weird start to my debut on Centre Court," Kendrick said, after which he was re-assured that the linesman (they don't name names at the All England Club), had recovered. "He was holding his chest, I didn't know what was going on. I was just ready to serve and heard this loud thump. I didn't know what to do."

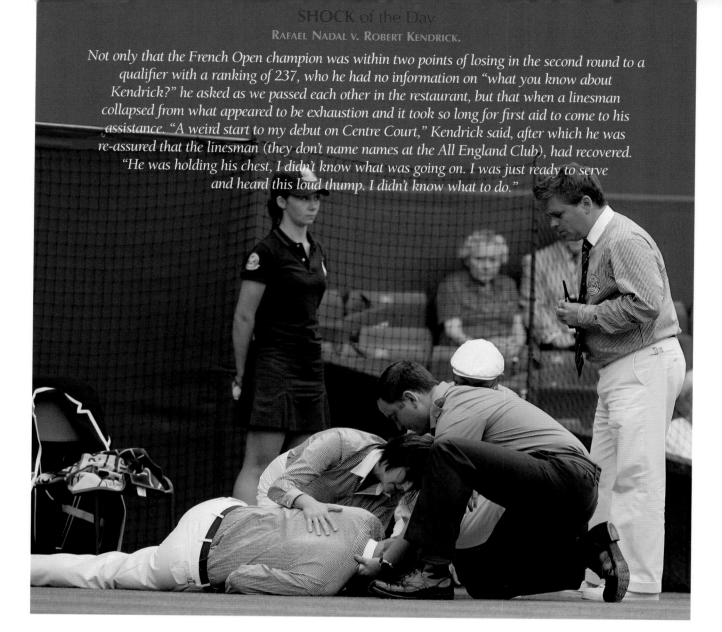

But, as we know, Murray does not like to think he cannot try anything he lends his hand to. He gritted and grinded his way back in the second, though was fortunate not to have trailed 4-1 when a call against Benneateau on a sideline was shown to be erroneous. Instead, Murray won eight of nine games, fashioning a series of supremely gifted winners, one running backhand pass on the first point of the tenth game the prelude to a love service hold that ought to have drawn all the spirit from the world No.55.

The points were beginning to become as drawn out as those that test the patience of a saint at Roland Garros. One 28-stroke rally in the sixth game of the second set was won by Benneteau with a superb backhand winner; but Murray clinched it, which went some way to underlining the composition of the afternoon. Then Benneteau, not put off when a pigeon flew across his eye-line as he prepared to serve, proved the steadier.

Roddick, who defeated Florian Mayer of Germany 6-4, 6-1, 6-2 said: "I wasn't that thrilled to go on a little after 7.30 but it felt right on the court tonight, I was aggressive and did what I wanted to do. I was reacting and playing and that felt normal which is welcome at this point." Roddick was beaten by Murray in the semi-finals of the San Jose tournament in February that marked the teenager's most vivid impression on the tour. He was asked whether he felt Brad Gilbert, who coached him to the US Open title in 2003, would be a decent fit for Murray. "Well, California and Texas (Gilbert's home and Roddick's) aren't that far apart but California and Ireland, that's different."

"I think you mean Scotland," someone said. "Oh, I've shot myself in the foot there," Roddick answered. The British contingent had to hope that on Friday afternoon, on Centre Court, the trend was not catching.

●

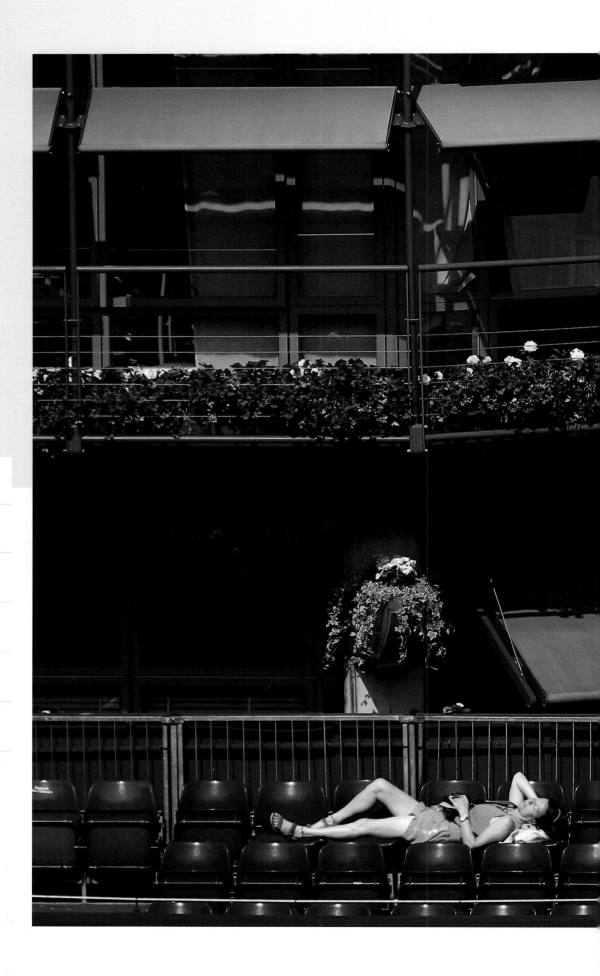

Day **FIVE**
30.06.2006

VERDASCO
VS
NALBANDIAN

FERRERO
VS
STEPANEK

DJOKOVIC
VS
YOUZHNY

HEWITT
VS
LEE

HINGIS
VS
SUGIYAMA

BLAKE
VS
MIRNYI

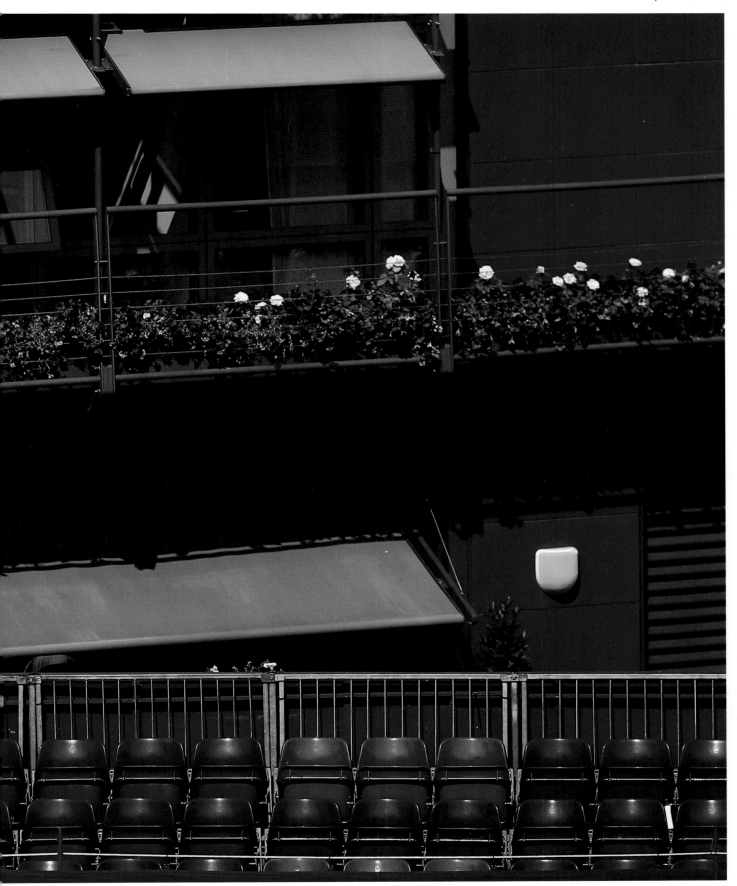

Juan Carlos Ferrero

Friday 30 June...

One of the marvellous aspects of the Wimbledon experience is the number of nooks and crannies from which you can watch the matches or, in some cases, bits and pieces of matches. Wandering the upper level of the player's restaurant on Friday, one's conversation was interrupted by a huge roar from the far reaches of the Club.

As one, it seemed, the crowd on Court No.13 had risen to acclaim Fernando Verdasco, the applause covered the grounds with a ripple effect, digging into the senses even of those watching Juan Carlos Ferrero against Radek Stepanek on the court immediately below the third-tier balcony. You couldn't actually see the shot that won it for Verdasco, or lost it for David Nalbandian, the No.5 seed from Argentina, but you knew the crowd had received the result it had wanted.

Strangely, given that he was a former runner-up, Nalbandian didn't seem to be as disturbed by the defeat as he should have been. He had actually asked if he could play first, so that he had time to watch the World Cup quarter final between Argentina and Germany later in the afternoon. But, having lost the first two sets on tie-breaks, had he thrown the third to make sure

Fernando Verdasco

David Nalbandian

Radek Stepanek

he had his feet up in front of the telly later? His monosyllabic response to questions afterwards said it might have been so.

He had clearly been distracted throughout. Having lost the first set on a tie break, he erupted. As Katie Scott in *The Times* reported: "Nalbandian picked up a warning for racket abuse and was alleged to have directed some colourful language towards disapproving fans. It is behaviour like this that has prevented him from becoming a true star of the game. He is the sort of player you would love to hate, if only you could muster the enthusiasm."

Verdasco, meanwhile, was in seventh heaven, reaching the last 16 of Wimbledon for the first time. So, too, had Stepanek, of the Czech Republic, regarded by Tim Henman, among others, as a genuine title contender, and Novak Djokovic of Serbia and Montenegro, the youngest player remaining in the draw and someone about whom British fans were going to hear an awful lot more. Djokovic's family had made representations to the Lawn Tennis Association, during the Davis Cup tie in Glasgow in April, keen to see what may be offered to them should ➤

Novak Djokovic

they decide, for the sake of Novak and his younger brothers, to move overseas.

Clearly, there were many more options available in Britain – the facilities at the new National Tennis Centre, sponsorship possibilities, being based in a hub like London – and the Djokovic clan were doing their best to talk up the advantages while knowing they could not afford to upset their mother nation. The more we saw of Djokovic, the player, the more we liked him. His 4-6, 6-2, 6-3, 6-3 victory over Mikhail Youzhny of Russia, was that of a very determined young man, apparently without nerves or indecision. The only trouble was the prospect of falling asleep waiting for his interminable bounces of a tennis ball before he served. 19 was the highest count.

The first Friday was also another day of completing unfinished business. Andy Murray's match against Julien Benneteau had to be concluded, as did that of Lleyton Hewitt, the 2002 champion, against Hyung-Taik Lee of South Korea. Hewitt had won the Stella Artois championship at Queen's Club for the fourth time, eight days before The Championships. He looked grooved, in touch with his game, ready to rock. But Lee, ranked 102, was a player who knew his way around a grass court and had a game of infinite touch. His one handed backhand was a match for anyone's.

Hewitt had struggled the previous evening. He had dug out the third set tie break from 6-3 down but, having served for the match, been pipped in the fourth, which, at well past 8 pm, led to the abandonment of play for the evening.

Mikhail Youzhny

Thus, we had the bonus of a one set play-off. Both players were keen to get the matter over with and asked to come back as first match, rather than play second, as was the norm.

The Australian was quicker from the blocks, held serve and was three points from a 2-0 lead but Lee responded, fired a couple of aces to hold again, and it became 4-4. There was a wonderful chance for Lee at 15-30 but he netted a relatively routine backhand as Hewitt struggled to regain ground. It could have been 15-40 but Hewitt saw the danger off with two aces of his own. Then he pounced. A beautiful forehand crosscourt winner took him to match point; Lee's netted forehand was a disappointing ending. "It was survival out there, that's all I can say," Hewitt said.

On Centre, Murray's match was also over in one set, probably his best of the tournament in what seemed onerous circumstances. Benneteau held his first service game to love and

subsequently lost six games in a row. Murray was through to the third round once again, where he would face Andy Roddick.

One of the more wondrous stories of the year had been the progressive comeback of Switzerland's Martina Hingis, a grand slam champion at 16, who had decided, in 2003, to take an indefinite break from the game.

She was troubled by the powerful influences all around her and by a debilitating foot injury that had led her to court action against the makers of her shoes. Hingis had done some television commentary, some horseback riding, and yet, she felt, something was missing. Ah! Competition.

At the start of the year, on the Gold Coast of Australia, she returned, without a ranking, and surrounded by pessimists. Surely, one still so small, could not hack it at the second time of asking.

But Hingis had never lacked for self confidence. She was back in the groove almost immediately, reaching the quarter finals of the Australian Open and trouncing Maria Sharapova at her following tournament, in Tokyo. In less than three months, she was back inside the top 20, which she had once held for 209 weeks.

In the third round, she was confronted with Ai ➤

Lleyton Hewitt (left)
Hyung-Taik Lee (below)

Ai Sugiyama

Sugiyama, of Japan, initially noted more for her doubles play (she had been ranked No.1 in doubles in 2000), but whose singles had improved demonstrably enough to have been inside the world's top 30 for the past five years. This would be tough, Sugiyama was not going to acquiesce easily.

It turned into a classic match – Hingis having to strain to win the first set, the dogged Japanese taking the second and then, apparently, running out of steam at the start of the third. Hingis led it 3-0.

She would win only one more game. "On this surface, Ai is probably harder to face than anyone else because she is so fast," Hingis said.

"Maybe because of my first two matches (Hingis had only dropped seven games), everyone was thinking I was going to go through easily. But she is a tough cookie, a strong survivor." Hingis was aghast to be confronted with a suggestion that her return had now reached a plateau, that the third round of Wimbledon constituted a failure. "I won the Italian Open, at the French I had a bad day of food and you cannot play Kim (Clijsters) if you are not 100 per cent. There are things I have to think about but, in the past, losses always made me stronger. I know what I have to work on to continue to progress."

Still, a certain element of gloss had gone out of the tournament, for Hingis retained an ability to coax the ball around a court with variations of subtlety and force. She was still a consummate rallier.

To lose to the 12th seed was a real blow. Sugiyama enjoying her win was a remarkably joyous sight.

QUOTE of the Day

"Andy Murray is making jokes of me like 'what's up team-mates, British,' or something like this. Especially Greg (Rusedski). Greg makes jokes with me every day. Every time I see him, he says: 'What's up, British.' It's nice, you know. We are really good friends and have fun. But these rumours, nothing serious really so far." Q: England v. Portugal in the World Cup tonight, who do you want to win? A: England

NOVAK DJOKOVIC OF SERBIA AND MONTENEGRO ON THE STORIES LINKING HIM WITH A MOVE TO BRITAIN

Martina Hingis

James Blake

Mentioning remarkable sights brings me to Nick Bollettieri wearing a suit. This is the archetypal sunshine man, the famed coach and president of the IMG Academy, where tennis and big business mix, but the emphasis is on bringing the best out of the youth fortunate enough to be offered a place at Nick's table. But, on this day, he was invited into the club's inner sanctum, so he had no choice but to don a tie. Bolletieri was writing for *The Independent* offering a distinctive insight. As such: "I was at Max Mirnyi's five-set win over James Blake and it was the most intriguing singles match I've seen here so far this year in terms of ebb and flow, strategic changes, attack and response, counter-attack, and ultimately, mental strength and a killer instinct.

"I believe the essence of Mirnyi's 6-4, 3-6, 4-6, 6-1, 6-0 victory could be found at two specific points where Max came out on top because of what I'll call the 'Mac Attack' strategy. The first was on the opening point of Blake's first service game in the fourth set, with the American leading two sets to one and Max 1-0 in the fourth, having served. Blake double-faulted. Why? For my money, because Max had started charging in on Blake's serve, and even though Blake was ahead, somewhere in his mind, this 6ft 5in giant opponent was running at him from then on, even when he was standing still.

"Blake feared Mirnyi coming in, and the physical manifestation was uncertainty, and a double fault. Max then chipped and charged, twice, for 0-40 then mixed it up by staying back hitting a winner from there. He had broken the serve, and he was back in it. The tide turned." Once the match went into a fifth set, the smart money was on Mirnyi, for Blake, despite being a top ten player, had not won a five setter in his career – the total had now reached a dispiriting nine.

Bye bye, James. ●

Max Mirnyi

EXPLANATION of the Day

MAX MIRNYI, *of Belarus, who defeated American, James Blake 6-4, 3-6, 4-6, 6-1, 6-0, on how he got the nickname 'The Beast'.* "It goes back ten years when David Rikl and I were travelling in Asia, playing some Challenger tours. Despite the fact we were staying in cheap hotels and not having dinner at times because places were closed and we didn't know what to do, I would still go out the next day and play tough matches. Win or lose, it didn't matter. He just started to say that I am The Beast. It stuck.

"Any headlines I make, it's not Max Mirnyi, it's The Beast. I think it's good that people have something to relate to. Later in my career, I picked up on some mixed doubles titles, after a while I teamed up with Anna Kournikova. Then it was another splash of information and something to talk about, because then there was 'Beauty and the Beast.'"

69

Day **SIX**
1.07.2006

AGASSI
VS
NADAL

MURRAY
VS
RODDICK

Saturday 1 July...

It was a tale of two matches. They involved two Americans, a Spaniard and a Scot and they had the effect of transforming the Wimbledon landscape.

The middle Saturday at the championship has been designated as "Chairman's Day" offering the prospect of stars from the world of sport and showbiz (what's the difference these days?) a Royal Box seat, an introduction, and a chance to savour the best of tennis fayre. Where else would you see Billy Bonds, the former West Ham United captain, sitting next to Bruce Forsyth, the doyen of song and dance men and talking as if they were long-time mates? Actually, I discovered later that they are!

When the initial programme for the middle Saturday was announced, there had been four matches on Centre Court but it dawned on the authorities that, as Stanislas Wawrinka of Switzerland and Croatia's Mario Ancic had taken two hours and ten minutes over two sets of grass court tennis on Friday evening, the chances of completing the schedule were severely compromised.

Andrew Jarrett, the referee, explained the *volte face*: "Unfinished matches by convention are scheduled for completion as second match the next day on the same court. As there is likely to be insufficient time today to complete the published Centre Court programme, I (the referee) have amended the Order of Play. The Wawrinka vs Ancic match will now be completed as second match on Court 1 and if the Court 1 programme is thereby put at risk of not finishing today the (Marcos) Baghdatis vs (Sebastien) Grosjean match may be played elsewhere, if necessary. It is vital for the players that all the singles matches are completed today, to avoid disadvantaging any player and to maintain the overall event programme. We always try to be fair to all competitors."

When the decision was made and revealed to the crowd on Centre Court, there was a gentle

**'Chairman's Day'
Stars from the world of
sport and showbiz.**

ripple of applause, probably because they feared it would mean Maria Sharapova being shifted elsewhere. Now the royals and the rebels could settle back and await the introduction of Andre Agassi and Rafael Nadal, the entrée to what would become the most sumptuous of banquets.

The Americans were already beginning to fear that this was not going to be their day. It turned out to be a shocker. As Wimbledon moved into its second week (the traditional break on Sunday meant it was alone in the grand slam camp), there was one American left in the men's or women's singles. That was Shenay Perry, an unseeded 21 year-old, ranked 62nd, who would ➤

Maria Sharapova

not be favoured against Russia's Elena
Dementieva. It would be Perry's first round-of-16
match in a grand slam tournament.

In the 84 years since The Championships
moved to their current location and the challenge
round was abolished, America had never had a
worse showing. It was a sign of the globalisation
of tennis that there were as many Poles,
Georgians, Cypriots, Finns, Chinese, and, yes,

even Britons in the fourth round as Americans.
Serbia, a country of approximately 10 million
people, had three players in the second week.
"That's really strange," said Jelena Jankovic, one of
their number.

The least of the surprises was, though, the
highest of dramas. The end of Agassi in SW19,
obliterated by a Nadal performance that was at
once stark and invisible. Nobody really saw

Agassi's Farewell – Winner of The Rolex Wimbledon
Picture of the Year Competition 2006

Rafael Nadal

Nadal, or cared to acknowledge the truth. His best moments drew only mild applause, his rare mistake giving fans a ray of hope. Such was the power of Agassi's charisma over the grounds during his 7-6, 6-2, 6-4 defeat.

American fans had needed not to totally embrace this farewell, for Agassi had scheduled to play the US Open in what was bound to be a swirl of emotion. In London, he wanted so badly to give ➤

them a taste of Borg, Sampras or Laver, but he just couldn't forestall the future. Nadal had arrived, on grass, sooner than anyone expected – himself included. He suddenly looked close to the finished product, given the natural limitations of his top-spin forehand and baseline dependency.

His serve confounded Agassi, probably the greatest instinctive returner of all time. His volleys, rare as they were, had some conviction.

He was completely unfazed by the low, punishing groundstrokes – Agassi delivered mightily on that score – because his strength, quickness and desire are such overriding factors.

"He moves so well that, even on grass, he doesn't get behind," Agassi marvelled. "It's not so much that he's running things down, being a punching bag, he can actually do things with it. He takes a lot but he gives a lot more. His movement is just out of this world."

As the first set entered a tiebreak, Agassi knew he had to win it. The 20 year-old Nadal was obviously just warming up, even in a heatwave that had the Centre Court patrons fanning themselves with their programmes and newspapers. The two were playing on even terms; even with three set points against him at 4-5, Agassi fought bravely to hold.

Only moments before the tiebreak, Agassi unleashed a down-the-line that landed at the convergence of both lines, as perfectly as the shot has ever been hit. Wearing a necklace of which the beads spell out "Daddy Rocks," courtesy of his four year-old son, Jaden, Agassi was transporting fans back to his memorable run in '92, when he shocked the fans with his all-white conservatism and wiped out Boris Becker, John McEnroe and Goran Ivanisevic to win the title.

This time, the list of Royal Box patrons was nothing less than stunning: Billie Jean King, Martina Navratilova, Steffi Graf (Agassi's wife), Maria Bueno, Margaret Court and Stan Smith, plus assorted sirs, dames, earls and duchesses. Somewhere in the group was Roger Bannister, the first person to run the mile in less than four minutes. There was a sense that Agassi, in this kind of company, might stop time altogether.

The set easily could have gone his way. Serving at 3-5 in the tiebreak, Nadal took a pratfall behind his serve – but Agassi botched his return and shouted in frustration. Then Agassi was broken on each of his two serves, first on a missed forehand and then on Nadal's sensational cross-court forehand winner on the run. With the set abruptly in his hands, Nadal hammered an ace down the middle.

They could have called it right there. Having just turned 20, Nadal is game for a five-hour shoot-out; that's a dream for him. Agassi, at 36, has to pick his spots. "You never like being out there ordinary," he said earlier this week, but there are times when he cannot escape it. Emerging wearily from one changeover with his baseball cap tilted back and a towel over his shoulder, Agassi could have passed for a film producer at some celebrity tournament in Palm Springs, about to unleash his serve against Ron Howard.

Two days ago, Nadal said his goal at Wimbledon was to "have a very good tournament in three or four years." Only the fourth round is at hand (he'll play Irakli Labadze on Monday), but he might be there already. "Today, I serve the best day in my career, for sure," he said. "In the warm-up, I was thinking I was gonna lose, easy.

Rafael Nadal

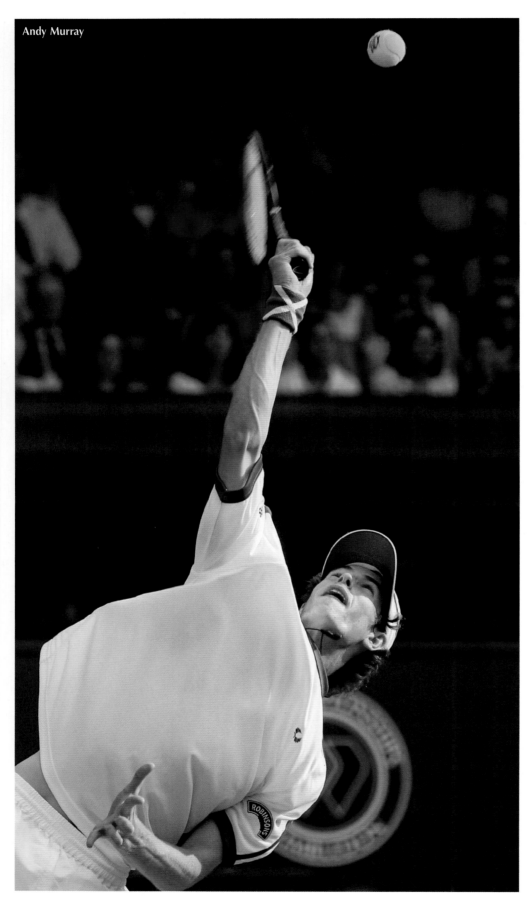

Andy Murray

ANDY MURRAY
VS
ANDY RODDICK

*Andy Murray beat Andy
Roddick 7-6, 6-4, 6-4.
The first set tie-break was
played at precisely the
same moment as England
were losing in a penalty
shoot out to Portugal in
the quarter final of the
World Cup. Occasionally,
one, then the other player,
had to pause as those
sitting on Centre Court
with ear-pieces, let out
muted roars and less than
muted sighs. Murray had
saved four set points
before the tie-break, the
second of which Roddick
should certainly have
converted, but he missed
a straightforward
forehand volley and then
flung himself across to
meet Murray's backhand
pass, when he could have
played the shot properly.
Murray took the
tie-break, played two
brutal forehand winners
to hold off break points in
the ninth game of the
second set and took that
with a stinging backhand
pass. Roddick was under
consistent pressure in
the third set, having to
survive break points
in three successive games,
before the two-time
runner up missed
a last, despairing
forehand and was on
his way home.*

Agassi was touching the ball unbelievable, very low, very tough. I can't return that. But in the match, is always different, no? This is so important for my confidence, for my belief that I can play good here."

Gracious to the end – a trait often overlooked in the young Spaniard – Nadal tempered the celebrations of his best shots and was reverential toward Agassi after the match, when the BBC broke with tradition and sent Sue Barker out to interview both players on court. "Andre is a legendary player," he said. "Unbelievable career. Today I play my best match, but is not my day to have good celebration. Is his day."

So many players have felt lost in retirement, haunted by the echoes of applause and unable to find an outlet for their competitive juices.

Agassi goes home to his beloved Steffi, who watched behind sunglasses with her usual detachment, and their two children. He has a strong circle of friends, a personally-created school for underprivileged children and a

QUOTE of the Day

I'm very disappointed. I'm not happy. I'm mad, whatever adjectives you want to throw in there, I'm not that smart so you think of them. It's not like me to lie down. I'll just keep trying to truck along, I just have to have faith that something good is going to happen sometime. It was pretty much all gravy for him.

ANDY RODDICK

foundation that has raised more than £40 million for inner-city children. Someone asked him a long, drawn-out question about second thoughts, whether a certain moment might have triggered a desire to reconsider his retirement, and his answer couldn't have been more clear: "No."

As for Wimbledon, he said, "This is where I learned how to respect the sport. To really appreciate what it means to play this game for a living. People work five days a week to play tennis on the weekend, and we get to call that a job. People sit here through tough, rainy conditions to see maybe a few minutes of play. They're out queuing up on the street for days. Just an unbelievable love of the sport.

"That's what separates this from every other event. To say goodbye, for me, means just as much as winning."

Then Andy Murray went out and beat Andy Roddick. Not just beat him but trounced him, in straight sets, emphatically, brilliantly, almost arrogantly. Didn't he do well? ●

Day **SEVEN**
3.07.2006

Monday July 3...

The day before Independence Day USA turned out to be that on which Wimbledon became independent of any American players – cue wailing, gnashing of teeth and scapegoat search – and Britain lost its independent spirit, Andy Murray, to an amalgam of presumptuous expectation and flagging resolve.

It was the hottest day of the tournament for sure – even Stefan Edberg, Sweden's Champion in 1988 and 1990 and one of the coolest men on the planet, had to take off his jacket and place it, a bit too nonchalantly if you ask me, across the front of the Royal Box, where he was seated next to Tony Pickard, his old mentor.

No doubt Pickard, a former Davis Cup international and captain, had plenty of views to share on Murray's performance as he has had on most things British tennis down the years, not least when Murray lost in straight sets to Marcos Baghdatis, a victory for the Cypriot that was the tennis-playing equivalent of holding your opponent at bay with your palm on his forehand and watching him thrash away, though you were always just out of reach.

The crowd still rallied behind the Scot, of course, determined to play its part as a kind of doubles partner, even though mildly confused about its rights to ownership. "Come on, Britain," someone shouted, keeping the support broad-based. Murraymania is a bit like its distant cousin, Henmania, but somehow more guttural in its utterances – and entirely without the silly hats.

There was, however, a black mark against the faithful when partisanship overstepped the mark, the crowd heatedly calling out a Baghdatis shot to the baseline, even as the ball remained in play and the rally continued. Most unsporting, and the crowd duly took a warning from the umpire.

QUOTE of the Day

"She's a really strange player, let's put it that way. She walk on the court. I don't think she really care about the way she play, she more care about how she look. She was touching her hair, her skirt. I was just thinking, if you don't want to play tennis, why are we even here trying hard? She took a towel here, she took a towel there. It's really annoying let's say."
RUSSIA'S ANASTASIA MYSKINA, HAVING BEATEN JELENA JANKOVIC, OF SERBIA, 6-4, 7-6.

Marcos Baghdatis and Andy Murray

It will be a points deduction next time, presumably, and after that, a fine.

It's a rare day, of course, when the crowd finds itself in deeper trouble with the authorities than Murray does. But, even the boy wonder's rap sheet lacked the energy and imagination that we are used to from this unashamedly temper-driven artist. The record will show that he was guilty of merely one sharp, bare-handed slap of his racket, one mimed throw of the same instrument, one bitter, but not prolonged, dispute over a line call with the umpire, and one slightly tetchy fling of a towel onto a line judge's nice, new Ralph Lauren jacket. At the time, incidentally, the jacket was hanging over the back of a chair and not over the back of the line judge. But that pretty much sums up the kind of disappointing afternoon Murray had.

The 19 year-old lost 6-3, 6-4, 7-6 and with him went Britain's last hope in The Championships, though he had taken one further step than 2005 in terms of rounds won and experience gathered. For some reason, he could not get himself going in the time honoured manner, there was no spring in his step, no snap in his delivery, too many false shots, especially the drop shot which he still played once too often (as I'm certain Pickard consistently whispered in Edberg's left ear).

"That wasn't good," Murray confessed. "It's got to be right up there with the worst I've returned serve all year. I've never missed so many second service returns, especially on my backhand. I just struggled." ➤

Stefan Edberg

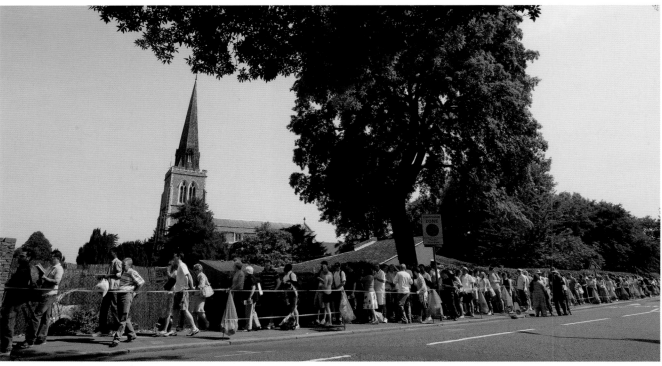

Maria Sharapova returns a
forehand to Flavia Pennetta

Maria Sharapova

"It's hard to explain. It has happened before but I need to cut these kind of matches out, especially in grand slams, because that's where you want to play your best tennis and you want to play better as the two weeks progress."

The seventh day of The Championships remained the must have ticket of the year. This is the only one of the four grand slam tournaments to play the round of 16, both men and women, on the same day. Perfect weather welcomed those striding down St Mary's Walk, in search of gold. You did not need a metal detector to discover it.

So much could happen, there were quarter finals at stake. For some this was perhaps their once in a lifetime opportunity. Flavia Pennetta, of Italy, was slightly better known as the girlfriend of the former world No.1 and French Open champion, Carlos Moya, than a potential grand slam challenger yet here she was on Court No.2, slugging it out toe-to-painted-toe with Maria Sharapova.

The only previous time they had met, in the Indian Wells tournament in 2004, Pennetta had taken Sharapova to three exacting sets, so chances were it would not be swift, either way. Sharapova didn't help herself with double faults in double figures. Pennetta, ranked No.48 on the Sony Ericsson WTA Tour, was powerful and secure off the ground but when Sharapova is struggling — and she definitely was — she somehow finds a way. "Flavia is just a solid, solid player," Sharapova said after her 7-6, 3-6, 6-3 victory. "She made me hit a lot of balls and whether I wasn't serving well or she was just too good, I didn't feel I served well enough today."

Survival, though, was a Sharapova maxim. It had been that of Nicola Vaidisova at the French Open, where the teenager from the Czech Republic, much like Sharapova in build, demeanour and character, came within touching distance of making the final. Vaidisova faced Na Li, the first Chinese to be seeded at The Championships. It was to be a profound experience.   ➤

Miss Li won the match 4-6, 6-1, 6-3 and when she was asked why she had won, she came up with the immortal sentence: "There is no reason for winning a match." In that case, we should put an end to the spuriousness of the press conference once and for all. Pardon me for differing with a grand slam quarter finalist, but Miss Li won because she played with a poise and certainty beyond her previous experience. It was a tremendously commanding debut at such a late stage in a grand slam and whether Vaidisova was tiring from her exploits in Paris or not – and she said she was 100 per cent, having withdrawn from Eastbourne – Miss Li deserved her victory most definitely.

As did Severine Bremond of France, formerly Severine Beltrame, a gorgeous girl from Montpellier in France, who had married her coach, Eric, the previous September. Having started The Championship ranked No.129, she was, wild card Agnieszka Radwanska of Poland, the 2005 girls' singles champion apart, the rank outsider. Now she was playing Ai Sugiyama, the Japanese fresh from victory over Martina Hingis in the third round.

Those early scuffles for a decent seat on Court No.13 were in for a treat as Mme Bremond saved nine set points to clinch the first set in a 13-11 tie-break which equalled the longest in the women's singles this year – Gisela Dulko, of Argentina, had taken the first set of the first round against Emma Laine of Finland after a similar marathon.

Sugiyama was sapped of energy and Mme Bremond went on to become the only non-seed in the last eight, winning 7-6, 6-3. ➤

Who would have wagered a nickel that the last American in the singles of either sex would be Shenay Perry, from Washington DC, who would celebrate her 22nd birthday on the 6th? Ranked No.62, she had reached the third round of Wimbledon the previous year but as the questions kept coming about why she was left to hold the Stars and Stripes, what was going wrong, the whole situation crowded in on her tennis.

She won only two games against Elena Dementieva, the seventh seed, saying: "This is a position I haven't been in before. It's a little nerve wracking. I'm just glad with what I accomplished."

Of the men's quarter finals, the most perplexing of all was that between Rafael Nadal, the No.2 seed and Irakli Labadze, of Georgia, not least for the body language of the two men. Well, in Labadze's case, just the body. His language was indecipherable.

On the Wednesday of the qualifying event, strolling the grounds of Roehampton, when one wasn't looking across at the development of the LTA's National Tennis Centre and wondering how many players we would need to produce to fill it, your attention was drawn to the doubles pair of Labadze and Vemic. Especially Labadze, who gave a whole new meaning to the term "portly".

It was remarkable to me that the pair qualified but even more that Labadze should reach the fourth round of The Championships with his girth. One could only assume that Mardy Fish, the American, retired after one set of their third round match because he was suffering from indigestion at the thought of losing to someone so round. But Labadze could strike the ball as if appearing not to move, though that would not work against Nadal, and he eventually lost in straight sets. There was, apparently, no truth to the rumour that he immediately joined the back of the queue for a Dutchee.

Only one non-seed would make the last eight in the men's and that was 34-year-old Jonas Bjorkman of Sweden who defeated his doubles partner, Max Mirnyi of Belarus, in five sets. "I had to play my best friend (Thomas Johansson) in the first round and Max in the fourth. We just tried to go out and may the best man win." With that, they would team up for a spot of men's doubles. And Bjorkman was still in the mix in the mixed. How would his body cope? ●

Shenay Perry

Day **EIGHT**
4.07.2006

DEMENTIEVA
VS
SHARAPOVA

MAURESMO
VS
MYSKINA

HENIN-HARDENNE
VS
BREMOND

Amelie Mauresmo

Tuesday 4 July...

Laurie Pignon had reported on the 1946 Wimbledon championships wearing his de-mob suit. Sixty years on, resplendent in members' tie – he had been invited to join the club in an honorary capacity in 1984 after his retirement as tennis correspondent of *The Daily Mail* and my foremost mentor – he was the perkiest 87-year-old imaginable. The twinkle in the eye had not faded. Nor had his love for women's tennis.

But something was upsetting him this women's quarter finals' day. He made his way to the Wimbledon press centre where, as usual, reporters and correspondents were dashing this way and that, articles to be furnished, previews to write, tales to tell, Robinsons to be quaffed.

There was not a whisky glass in sight, which is why Pignon – surnames were the rage among his peers and that's the way it stayed – didn't hang around too long.

Long enough though to set off on a tirade about Maria Sharapova or, more specifically, the noise made by Maria Sharapova. "Can't hear

Elena Dementieva

Maria Sharapova

myself think, old boy," Pignon muttered. "I remember (Billie-Jean) King playing (Virginia) Wade once in the seventies, King had her knee strapped and made a couple of grunting noises as she went for difficult shots and Wade complained to the umpire. It's changed now.

"Bloody nuisance, shouldn't be allowed, the air conditioning has gone in the members, so we're having to sit there with all the windows and ➤

QUOTE of the Day

Q: Going back to the grunting, do you think you're louder now than you ever were? A: What newspaper are you from? Q: The Daily Mail A: Oh, I thought it was The Sun. Q: Do you think you're louder or not? A: Are you partners in crime with the radio man on your right? It's such a pointless question. I always have the same answer to this question. I've done this ever since I started playing tennis and I'm not gonna change. This question only ever comes up at Wimbledon when you guys have all your Suns and Daily Mails and all that.

Kim Clijsters

doors open. Can still hear her. When's someone going to invoke Rule 26?"

That was the one that dealt with any unfair hindering of an opponent – and we didn't mean the momentary invasion of the court by a male streaker which caused both players to take their eyes off the ball.

Pignon was not the only person on Centre Court on the eighth day who felt the rule was being openly flouted. Maybe Elena Dementieva, Sharapova's fellow Russian, did not consider herself to be into the match enough to make an issue of the distraction, or that if she kicked up a fuss it would seem like sour grapes.

There surely had to come a time, though, when someone would complain.

"Personally, I think it's a little too much," – Dementieva, who lost 6-1, 6-4 to Sharapova, said. "But that's the way she has played for a long time and if the tour has allowed her to do such noise, it's...I think the umpire should calm her down a bit. We cannot control how loud she will scream the next day and the next day. I think the best way is to beat her, not to tell her what to do."

Those journalists trying to sneak "Grunt-o-meters" into Centre Court might have made better use of the statistics sheets which informed us that Sharapova had accumulated 20 unreturnable serves, which had a lot more to do with the reason she was into another Wimbledon semi-final. "I was very happy with what I did today, I try not to let things bother or distract me," Sharapova said. "There could be many things going on around the world but when I'm on the court, it's my job to get it done the best way I can. You can't feel great all the time."

Of the four quarter finals, three would be won in straight sets, Kim Clijsters and Justine Henin-Hardenne settling for another all-Belgian grand slam meeting – the 20th time in all tournaments they had squared up, but their first at Wimbledon – with fairly amenable wins over Na Li and Severine Bremond respectively. It was Amelie Mauresmo, the No.1 seed, who would be given the greatest scare. Almost all of it self-inflicted.

Mauresmo won the first set 6-1 against Anastasia Myskina and all in the French rose garden was blooming marvellous. Her coach,

Loic Courteau, settled back into his seat – as if any coach of Mauresmo was ever "settled" – and she came out for the second as if she had slipped into another person's body at the change of ends. Courteau could not believe he was watching the same player, something he was at a loss to explain later. Myskina, taken apart in the first set, was allowed a foothold in the match.

"What I had been doing, I wanted to do even more, but instead, I tried to force the match and started to make unforced errors, especially on the returns of serve. I had to step back a little bit at the end of the second set and find my rhythm again," said the Frenchwoman. Once re-discovered, Myskina was bundled out 6-1, 3-6,

6-3. Upstairs on the players' lawn, she dissolved into tears, for she really thought this might be her big Wimbledon break.

Mauresmo would, therefore, play Sharapova, but it was the prospect of Henin-Hardenne meeting Clijsters once more that really engaged the mind. They had met twice in the past month but their 18th meeting at tour level, the French Open semi-final, was much the more sad, Clijsters losing for the fourth time in succession in grand slam tournaments, a 6-3, 6-2 defeat at the end of which she barely brushed cheeks with her compatriot, barely brushed hands with the umpire, and brushed aside an attempt by Nelson Montfort, French TV's genial on-court inquisitor, to extract a few words.

To say Clijsters was depressed with her performance, given the circumstances and the opposition, is understating how badly she fell away under the depth and pugnacity of the defending Champion's performance. As the second set drifted away, Clijsters did not look terribly perturbed – at one stage she totally missed a smash as Henin-Hardenne tried to regain her balance after stumbling in the dust.

For seven games it was an edge of the seat affair but, thereafter, seats were flicking back into their closed positions and the crowd lost interest. A shame really because there was a different edge to the match, with the pair re-united as team-mates in the Fed Cup team by Carl Maes, the

Belgian captain, ten years after they had won the European under-14 event in Lee-on-Solent, with him as the coach, .

In the intervening years, they drifted apart, beset by their own growing pains and personal upheavals to the extent that the Belgian media preyed on their differences and drove a wedge between them.

Only when they each received a personal letter from Maes a couple of months ago, in which, written in Fleming and French (with an enclosed picture of those happy Hampshire days) he inspired them to let bygones by bygones and not let enmity rule, did they agree to play together again. The result? They defeated Russia, the ➤

holders, in the first round, and would be team-mates against the USA, in Ostend, the week after Wimbledon.

"We have talked a lot about that," Henin-Hardenne said after her 6-4, 6-4 victory over Mme Bremond of France. "We have been very professional adults. There's a lot of respect between us, that's it and it is very important."

Clijsters was asked to characterise her relationship with Henin-Hardenne. "We get along," she said. "People automatically want to create tension or something. I don't know about her, but I've never had that. To me, results don't matter at all. I like to make friends on the tour and knowing that, when I stop, I'll still be able to call the girls, meet and catch up. That's the thing I prefer to take away. We all want to win, but to me, that's more important than winning."

And Martina Hingis was still in town, not to play, but to watch. Her current beau, Radek Stepanek, of the Czech Republic, was preparing for his quarter final against Jonas Bjorkman. "She's a great person," he said. "I am happy in every way, the way I am playing, the way I am working, I am 100 per cent commited to my tennis and I am happy in my private life, too. When it comes to picking somebody to have in your heart, to be there with you, it is very important. It doesn't matter if you are a tennis player or not." ●

Amelie Mauresmo is congratulated by Anastasia Myskina after Mauresmo had won their match

Amelie Mauresmo

Day **NINE**
5.07.2006

HEWITT
vs
BAGHDATIS

NIEMINEN
vs
BJORKMAN

FEDERER
vs
ANCIC

Wednesday 5 July...

In the gloaming of a day that had been disrupted by intermittent rain and covered in ominous darkness, the lights went out on Lleyton Hewitt's 2006 Wimbledon challenge. It was extinguished by a remarkably bravura performance from Marcos Baghdatis, the radiant livewire from Paramytha, a coastal village in Cyprus.

His mother, Andry, could barely look, peering through the fingers of both hands as her 21 year-old son moved with ever increasing certainty towards a semi-final date. The light may have been fading but there was no diminution in the levels of Baghdatis' play. As he walked back from the chair with a 5-2 lead in the fourth set and Hewitt to serve, the smile on Baghdatis' face was one of "this is just *wonderful*– but I'm not sure it's actually for real."

A few points later and reality was crowding in, for Hewitt, the 2002 Champion, was walking towards him, having flicked off of his baseball cap and shaken his hair in the time honoured manner, offering a hearty handshake and a genuine word of congratulation. You could see in the Australian's eyes that he meant every word. Baghdatis may have been laughing too loudly inside to hear them.

"In as much as Baghdatis had a claim to fame," wrote Giles Smith in *The Times*, "it was in both beginning and ending the list of Cypriot greats of the postwar tennis era." Those of us fortunate enough to have been in Australia in January to witness the saving of the event by Baghdatis – for

Lleyton Hewitt

though Roger Federer won the title, it was the stubbly-faced, perma-smiley one who dragged it up by its shoelaces – were not surprised.

Continuing where he left off against Andy Murray in the previous round, the Cypriot did not so much launch an attack on Hewitt as commence a military operation designed to pound the No.6 seed into the dust. It has been noted of Baghdatis that he "plays with a smile" which, in the determindly grim-faced world of tennis, tends to be the code for "looks destined to be a massive under-achiever." But it became clear, during this match, that his smile emerged only at times of genuine self-amusement and that beneath his permanently crooked bandanna lurked a game-face that was ruthlessly serious.

Until deep into the second set, it did not seem like the genuine Hewitt out there but another of those tiresome court invaders who happened to resemble the Australian. He lost his first two service games of the match but, as the second set, too, looked destined to slip away, the bogus Hewitt was, metaphorically, led away by security and the real one stood up.

At last, familiar Hewitt shots began to flow, the huge, whipped forehands in which the racket appears in danger of going all the way round behind his head and re-appearing over his right shoulder and the ferocious double-fisted backhands, for which he gets down so low his knees practically graze the turf. He took the second set, both players were in full flow and the third set was, accordingly, a scrap, Baghdatis producing the shot of the match – an inhumanly ➤

quick service return – to win the tie-break. He wrapped up a place in the semi-finals for the loss of only two games in the fourth. The Baggy camp was delirious.

Everybody Loves Marcos. Garry Richardson, the BBC interviewer with a reputation for bruising inquisition and certainly not given to fawning, was taken aback to receive a text from Baghdatis, giving his address, the time when he would be ready for an interview and 'look forward to seeing you.' Hewitt could be a lot more disarming than his reputation indicated but few neutrals in the crowd were on his side.

"I haven't seen a lot of him play (Hewitt didn't exactly thrill at the prospect of turning on his TV to watch Baghdatis in the final of the Australian Open in January), but to his credit, he didn't give me too many cheap points out there. Every game ➤

Marcos Baghdatis

I was in, he came up with something. There was a service game where I had game point at 0-3 and he comes up with three unbelieveable shots in a row to end up going up a double break. The following game, I have 0-40 and he comes up with a few big serves. A case of missed opportunities."

For Baghdatis, having been in a state of physical distress in the first round, a place in the semi-finals was an astonishing achievement. The story of his parents' decision to send him away, at 14, to the Patrick Mouratoglou academy in Paris had to be re-told, how a boy who so loved the home life in Cyprus could only learn what it would take to be a real player if he was sent abroad, where he would cry himself to sleep in the evenings because he was so lonely.

To see the family now – knowing how deeply they had felt their separation – made one's own eyes well.

"All the coaches I had believed in me so much and helped me so much," Baghdatis said. "This is the way I am, this is who I am. I love this game. I love playing in front of so many people. At the beginning I went out believing that I can win, of

Jonas Bjorkman

course. I beat a lot of good players this year and the years before. But in the middle of the second set (where he had come to a juddering halt against Roger Federer in the Melbourne final), I'm one set and two break points up against Hewitt, I'm playing for the Wimbledon semi-finals and, so I start to think a bit, start choking a bit." The choke didn't last long.

Baghdatis would have to wait to discover who his semi-final opponent would be, for the second match on Court No.1, between Rafael Nadal and Jarkko Nieminen, the Finn, was held over because it had taken Jonas Bjorkman and   ➤

Mario Ancic

Radek Stepanek so long to fulfil their quarter final obligations. Four hours and three minutes to be exact.

But what a finale.

He hugged himself but it was meant as a gesture that Bjorkman wished he could have hugged everybody on No.1 and, had they released him from the club grounds with immediate effect, there would not have been a person safe in Wimbledon Village from the Swede's clutches.

Bjorkman was in love with the world – not just Petra, his wife, and Max, his young son, and why wouldn't he be? A place in only his second grand slam semi-final, nine years after Greg Rusedski pipped him at the post, in five sets, to reach the US Open final was his, and if the task was as daunting as it came – playing Roger Federer on grass in the full glare of his imperiousness – Bjorkman regarded it as a treasurable opportunity.

The only men in the field who had played more consecutive Wimbledons were Rusedski and Andre Agassi, so Bjorkman was carrying the hopes and dreams of all those who, once they

reach 30 in tennis are all too hastily condemned as yesterday's men. His 7-6, 4-6, 6-7, 7-6, 6-4 victory over Stepanek required the Swede to save two match points in the fourth set and resist Stepanek's prancing, feisty fightback in the fifth.

Earlier this year, Bjorkman asked Thomas Johansson, his compatriot and good friend, if he would mind sharing Todd Woodbridge as a coach.

Johansson said he was cool with that and, in the first round here, Bjorkman beat him in four sets. As he prepared to confront the world No.1, he would have covered more ground than most and the feeling was mounting that the opposition was doing more than its fair share to help Federer across the finishing line to his fourth consecutive title.

Tim Henman – a veritable sapling at 31 – required five sets to defeat Robin Soderling in the first round and was beaten in straight sets by Federer in the second; Nicolas Mahut, of France, played seven sets to reach his third round appointment and went the same way; Tomas Berdych had played two five-setters in preparation for crossing the Swiss in the fourth

round. He was pole-axed. Of his four run-outs before the Centre Court swatting he received from Federer, Mario Ancic had been extended longer each time. For the Champion, there had been five matches, 15 commanding sets – a piece of cake with a cherry on top.

Bjorkman was the oldest man to reach this stage at Wimbledon since Jimmy Connors in 1987. He put it down to the handful of pills he was taking before every match to numb the pain of inflammation in his serving arm. "But it's so much fun to be out here, I may not have too many Wimbledons left and this is such a special tournament, the greatest one," he said.

Federer's victory over Ancic – the one which made him really believe he would win the title again – was recorded thus by the incomparable Simon Barnes: "The rain fell and the rain stopped, and the rain fell and the rain stopped and Federer got stronger and Federer got stronger and in the end there was no room for doubt in anyone's mind.

"If there had been any outside my own imagination, it now lay buried beneath a glorious precipitation of rainbows." ●

Day **TEN**
6.07.2006

**KNOWLES &
NAVRATILOVA
VS
RAM &
ZVONAREVA**

**MAURESMO
VS
SHARAPOVA**

**CLIJSTERS
VS
HENIN-HARDENNE**

**NADAL
VS
NIEMINEN**

**A Champion's Final
Curtain – Martina
Navratilova and Mark
Knowles lose to Andy
Ram and Vera Zvonareva**

Thursday 6 July...

She would be 50 in October and that she was on court at all was testament to all Martina Navratilova had meant and would continue to mean to Wimbledon. But this was it, the end of the playing line for a champion in every sense of the word.

Who could argue with these SW19 statistics? Nine singles titles, seven ladies doubles titles, and four mixed doubles titles – tying the record of Billie Jean King – amid a career accumulation of 167 singles titles, 174 in doubles and over 1,400 total wins. The last match she would play in her favourite tournament was not perhaps the finest, a 7-5, 6-1 defeat in the third round of the mixed doubles in partnership with Mark Knowles. They were beaten by Andy Ram of Israel and Vera Zvonereva of Russia. Martina called it "a terrible way to go, probably the worst it could possibly be."

Of course, she would have liked the finale to come on Centre Court, the scene of so many of her finest days but the schedule would not permit it. Eye witnesses said that Navratilova left the court 'with head bowed and bottom lip quivering. The autograph hunters were to be disappointed. She did not stop for a look around the court.'

She managed a smile later but there was a sadness too. "Now that I'm collecting my AARP (American Association of Retired Persons) discount, it's time to move on with life," she said. "I want to spend more time with my animals, devote more to my businesses, I'm running the Rainbow Card, which raises money for gay and lesbian organisations in the United States, I want to spend more time on that and I want to do some commentating, if somebody wants to listen to what I've got to say."

There had never been a dull moment when Navratilova was around, not least because she had made a definitive impact on the sport, waking it up to the developments in physique and diet that have had a profound effect but, most importantly, never straying from her belief in the wonders of serve and volley, of grace at the net, of making a stand.

It was still hard to believe that the next time we would see her at Wimbledon, it would probably be in the Members' Enclosure.

But time goes on. Amelie Mauresmo had celebrated her 27th birthday on the day before the women's semi-finals. Her opponent was Maria Sharapova, who always came to life when Wimbledon beckoned. Mauresmo had never been to a final here but, after three losing semi-finals in the past four years, there was a feeling of her turn.

And yet almost everyone on Centre Court watching the match was getting themselves geared for the moment that Mauresmo would shoot herself in the foot. It was not as if she hadn't blown away her toes before, though winning the Australian Open – circumstances notwithstanding – had done wonders for her often crooked self-belief.

Amelie Mauresmo

It became a dramatic, beautiful, infuriating match, in which brilliance alternated with wince-inducing error, each players alternately inspired and then overwhelmed by the grandeur of the occasion. In fact, Mauresmo won the first set by the unexpected tactic of playing the better tennis. She is a lovely player to watch, a game full of variation, or light and shade, with a one-handed backhand that's a wonder to behold for as long as she is playing loose, and self-forgetting.

The shrieking of Sharapova is more a territorial thing. It is a claim to ownership of the court – this is my place and I'll behave anyway I want. And she feeds off a weakness better than anyone

QUOTE of the Day

We can definitely hear the (Sharapova) screams. That's Wimbledon for you, it's like a funfair. She's got a powerful voice. It's a nuisance, but we put up with it.

HARRY COOPER,
SOMERSET ROAD RESIDENT

4-0 in the final set, how would she play? Her serve was broken, inevitably she lost the next game, was pushed to the limit to hold but came up with some brilliant serving and then took the game back to the Russian. When she won, her leap would not have shamed Dame Nanette du Valois. "I've got a tremendous picture, my finest of the event," John Cassidy, *The Times* photographer announced and there it was on the back page next morning, in all its glory.

"I'm taking every loss as a new beginning," Sharapova said. "These things teach me a lot. I'm gonna go back on the court and I'm gonna work. Talk is cheap, I've just got to do it. Now I'm gonna go out on a shopping spree, I do that every year."

If she wanted a pleasant companion in the West End, Kim Clijsters was now free. The all Belgian semi-final had gone the way of their past four meetings in grand slams, with Justine ➤

Maria Sharapova

else in the women's game, and so, when Mauresmo was having her "I'm in front, oh heavens, I might win" moment, Sharapova dug back into the match.

Mauresmo took a comfort break and it worked. She reeled off four successive games, giving her opponent no pace to feed on, causing Sharapova to miss and miss again, which forced her to long, doleful looks to the box where her father, Yuri, dark glasses in place, winced.

'Even Amelie can't lose it from here.' That's what people in the press box were saying. To which the reply was something akin to 'she can lose from anywhere, just look at her CV.' So at

John Inverdale of the BBC: "Right, it's your turn to ask us some crazy questions now." Auckland: "Is that a fake tan?"

Justine Henin-Hardenne and Kim Clijsters

Henin-Hardenne emerging triumphant because it looked as if she wanted it that little bit more. Though a break up in each set, she could not sustain her advantage, Henin-Hardenne stepping up her play when required to win 6-4, 7-6.

"I gave her a lot of my better game and that's what I'm happy about," Clijsters said. "Losing to her in some of the other grand slams, my regret was that I didn't really give her my best. I felt like today, she had to work for it. That is the positive I can take away from this match. Hopefully, if everything goes according to plan, I'll be back here next year but that is something nobody knows for sure."

Across on Court No.1, the delayed men's quarter final between Rafael Nadal and Jarkko Nieminen was played out, and, as was becoming the norm on grass, Nadal won the points that really mattered. That morning, I had chatted with Nadal on the Wimbledon lawn, after his name had been carried in a French newspaper as among those athletes being tracked in a doping investigation in Spain. He was two matches away from a final which would be the story to end all tennis stories and his calm was shattered by an allegation that bit into his core.

"I feel bad that people would ever doubt me, because if they see the person I am, on the court and off the court, they know I am a fair person," he said.

Nadal proclaimed his innocence in a manner of semi-bewilderment and semi-fury. He described those who named him – but would not put their names to the article – as cowards and thieves. The thief analogy was that someone would steal the 20-year-old's integrity, make off with his good name. The world No.2 did not understand why anyone with no proof could be allowed to smear him and not give a jot for how it affected him. "It is so sad for me," he said.

"To be accused specifically of something I have never done and would never do in my life, it is hard to accept for me as an individual and for tennis as a sport. It is a pathetic story, one that shows a complete lack of respect. There is no doubt that the person who wrote this is a very bad person.

"It hurts more because the story is always the same – people doubt those who are winners, and think they must be cheating instead of accepting that they have the desire and the ability to win. I would prefer to lose than to win by cheating. I always fight 100 per cent in my matches and when I lose, I accept that defeat. I have heard these stories about other players as well but how can it be, when we are all tested so many times in a year – 18, 20 times?

Justine Henin-Hardenne

Rafael Nadal

Jarkko Nieminen

"The only reason I would be slightly worried on the day before a Wimbledon quarter final is if I had the tiniest doubt, but there is zero doubt. I am totally focused on my tennis. They can try to distract me, but they cannot do it. I am at complete ease with myself because I have never done anything and never will."

The Spanish Sports Ministry issued a statement saying it "denied categorically any implication of football or tennis players, Spanish or foreign, in the cited operation. The Ministry demands maximum respect and rigour in all publications and information around this process, to guarantee the rights of the affected persons and to avoid speculation about sportsman who have nothing to do with the investigation. At the same time, we consider it absolutely unfortunate the information in a French newspaper that speculates, without any evidence, on a number of footballers and even mentions the name of a tennis player."

All Nadal wanted to do was to get on with playing. A semi final against Marcos Baghdatis awaited and he loved the idea of that.

Day **ELEVEN**
7.07.2006

FEDERER
VS
BJORKMAN

NADAL
VS
BAGHDATIS

The two minute silence in honour of the lives that were lost in last year's London bombings

Roger Federer

Friday 7 July…

"You and Jonas are friends. As the match is unfolding, do you allow yourself any pangs of sympathy?" "No, not in the semis. Sorry."

Thus answered Roger Federer in the immediate aftermath of his 6-2, 6-0, 6-2 semi-final victory over Jonas Bjorkman, the most one-sided match at this stage of The Championships since the first recorded assimilation of records in 1922. "It was just a beautiful feeling," Federer said though, of course, Bjorkman did not share the emotion.

At its conclusion, Federer tossed one of his sweatbands into the Centre Court crowd and, as it was noted later, its flight did not appear to be weighed down by undue amounts of sweat. The route of the Swiss to the final was absolutely without concern, he had made a victory at such a juncture seem more like a first round encounter with a jumpy wild card.

The most poignant fact of this annihilation was that Bjorkman did not actually play badly. He did not carelessly dump his serve or keep hitting returns at the umpire's chair. In fact, he was composed, consistent and even aggressive against someone who, less than a decade before, had asked if he might practise with him and then remembered that he used to tank his practices.

"Yeah, there were some days I wasn't really in the mood to practise, especially not with Jonas because he was always so intense and I didn't enjoy that. I came on court just hoping for an easy hit. You wouldn't get that with him."

Times had changed, and intensity levels, though Bjorkman still pumped himself up to levels that were good enough when he played most people on grass. This was a different story. "Any player who intended to insert himself in front of the Federer runaway train yesterday would have had to be some kind of superhero," wrote Giles Smith in *The Times*. "Suitably caped and equipped with a Bjorkcave, a Bjorkmobile and a Bjorkcopter and maybe someone alongside in the role of Robin, he might, perhaps, have advanced to break point at some moment."

Unfortunately for this highly personable Swede, such a situation was for comic books. This was reality and the reality of a break point never materialised. Federer was in a class of his own, in an aura of his own, doing what he wanted to do without pause for an opponent's consideration. He was simply immense. In reaching another final, he had conceded a mere 52 games and dropped serve twice. "I had high expectations to win this match today," Federer ➤

Jonas Bjorkman

Rafael Nadal

www.wimbledon.c

95

mph

IBM

said. "I mean, I was flawless. I thought it was great. I'm very pleased. There's not much more I can say about it."

There was a not an awful lot more to be said about the second semi-final – Rafael Nadal against Marcos Badghdatis. Nadal was playing in what he described as "an incredible motivation." Baghdatis was one step away from his second grand slam final in six months.

From the outset, this time, he didn't seem to be able to believe where he was.

Three errors in the first game of the match and he was a break down.

In a flash, that had gone to 4-1 and, with a third service break, 6-1. Nadal led the second set 1-0 and was 0-40 on the first Baghdatis service game. Was this going to be a second rout? Then Nadal hesitated, struck a forehand long, could not return a forceful Cypriot serve, was undone by a forehand winner and then Baghdatis popped in another unreturnable serve. Whereas, they had been muted before, the Baggy choir began to shout. ➤

It didn't need much for Baghdatis to rouse himself and for the first time, at 3-3, he had a break point. Nadal's response said much about him, a crunching forehand, all wicked spin and placement, that Baghdatis could just get a racket to, prompting a fierce overhead winner. In the 16-point tenth game, Baghdatis denied the Spaniard a couple of set points, the first with a beautiful inside out forehand (what courage!) and the second, having opened up the court, a

Marcos Baghdatis

forehand volley into the Nadal forehand corner.

But, having to play consistently with what seemed like his back to the wall, would clearly take a toll. Against Nadal, every point had to be earned; you got owt for nowt. The stress on body and mind was immense and, consequently, Baghdatis found himself facing two more set points in the 12th game, the first of which he saved, the second he could not, as Nadal fashioned a miraculous forehand winner and went on one of his leaping charges across the court. Baghdatis knew what it meant.

Unable to take one of two break points in the first game of the third set, the bounce had seemed to leave the Cypriot legs, even though he had completed his quarter final a day before Nadal. The Spanied settled the set and his 6-1, 7-5, 6-3 victory with compelling assurance. He had survived nine break points in the match, which went to the heart of his competitive fires. "All I have to do now (against Federer)" he said, "is play the best match of my career."

Nadal had not dropped serve since the second set of the second round against Robert Kendrick, the back of Centre Court resembled more the consistency of clay than grass, there had been a subtle shift in his service action, for Nadal was tossing the ball considerably further into the court and cracking it. Remarkably, Nadal had made more advances to the net than Federer to reach the final.

There was a frisson around the grounds as people contemplated the prospect of yet one more Federer/Nadal meeting. Jimmy Connors, twice a former Champion and now settling ever more comfortably into the commentator's chair, was moving to its edge bit by bit. "Nadal has the eyes, he has the look," Connors said. "And sometimes attitude plays just as big a part as the tennis itself.

"Who is going to take a risk when we least expect it? I'm from Missouri – the Show Me State – so I'm waiting for Federer to show me that he has it in him to stay one step ahead of this guy. Clay is not his surface and I'm proud that he took the game to Nadal in Paris and played the kind of tennis he did. A lot of guys could not do that.

"Hell, I'm one of them.

"Now we have the other side of the coin. If Nadal goes into the final thinking he's just happy to be there, he should stay at home. With his attitude, I can't see that happening. If they play the tennis we expect, it will be a wonderful showpiece. Nadal's made the change-up on grass, he's moved inside the baseline, he's unafraid to come to the net. It is a long time since Wimbledon has been this electric." ●

CONFUSING ANSWER
of the Day

Q: When it rains, does that ever worry you? A: Yeah, sure no? Is boring, no? I am in the locker room, waiting. I come to the here outside in the grass. Yeah, outside here. So, no, not a lot of things I can do, no, because today I can't go to the home, because I am not practising before. So I am waiting.

Very good patience, no?

RAFAEL NADAL

Rafael Nadal celebrates

127

Day **TWELVE**
8.07.2006

MAURESMO
VS
HENIN-HARDENNE

BRYAN &
BRYAN
VS
SANTORO &
ZIMONJIC

B. BRYAN &
WILLIAMS
VS
RAM &
ZVONEREVA

Saturday 8 July…

Roger Federer walked out of a television studio – where the producers had, for some inexplicably Gallic reasoning, asked him to throw some clothes in the air and make sure they landed on his head – and Amelie Mauresmo followed him in. "He's a genius," she whispered. "I can't imagine that I have the same ranking as him."

The tables did not lie then and they did not lie on Wimbledon women's singles finals day. The occasion of her brushing shoulders with Federer was a day before the French Open in May, and the last time a French woman had been feted with the No.1 ranking in Paris was Suzanne Lenglen, (le grande dame) eight decades earlier. The last French woman to win Wimbledon was the self-same Suzanne, the last of her six titles in 1925.

On the morning of the Wimbledon final, my thoughts went back six weeks, to chasing Mauresmo through the throng at Roland Garros, wanting to capture her thoughts on what it was like for the Australian Open champion, a French woman, to try to take that into the French championships, where everything had played notorious tricks. ➤

Justine Henin-Hardenne

When the chair on which she was to be interviewed collapsed underneath her and she handed its seat to her minder, she couldn't help but see the the incident's amusing side. Was this a new, freer Mauresmo? Walking through the grounds of a place where she was once filled with dread, it was with the air of an athlete who was in the prime of life and in complete control.

After her success in Australia, Mauresmo flew straight home to compete in the Open de Gaz in Paris. "It was like a celebration of me," she said. "The crowd was unbelieveable. I didn't know whether I would be able to give a good account of myself because I was tired after Australia but match by match I felt so good on the court. I really want to find that certain same emotion here as at the French because it makes you feel so strong. If I can get that adrenalin again..."

Things were bound to have been different this year. When she was a maiden, in grand slam winning terms, she was looked upon by the French especially as vulnerable, the crowd even preyed on what they perceived as her weakness under pressure. The emotion of the occasion really got to her. Since a shattering third round defeat to Ana Ivanovic, the Serbian

No.29 seed in January, Mauresmo had won the Sony Ericsson championships in Los Angeles and followed that with a comprehensive demolition of the field in Melbourne.

"I pride myself that I was the strongest player out there (at the Australian)," she said. "If I lost a set, I said to myself 'oh well, you start again, you can do it.' Now I have the privilege of being the No.1 player. I feel I have achieved my goals, the pressure may be here but it is a little bit off my shoulders, I have nothing more to prove. I don't know how it will be on the court here, there is some tension in the air, that is to be expected but it is not a tension I can't handle. I do have to convince myself that I am the No.1 player – as a kid that was my dream and now it has happened I really don't know what it feels like. I have no idea how I can tell you. I just believe I have the answers to all the questions within me."

The French Open came and went in its usual manner for Mauresmo, she was beaten in the fourth round by Nicola Vaidisova of the Czech Republic, beat a retreat to England, but lost in her first round match in Eastbourne. What could we possibly have expected at Wimbledon? The final? Why not?

Justine Henin-Hardenne was aiming to become the 10th woman of all time to complete a grand slam of major titles and the first Belgian to win Wimbledon. There was sure to be a 16th different woman champion in the Open Era and it was the first time since 1971 that the Wimbledon final would feature the winner of the Australian and French Opens – when Evonne Goolagong, who had won in Paris, defeated Margaret Court 6-4, 6-1. Court would discover the following month that she was pregnant with her first child.

No such surprises – unless unplanned – were expected of the 2006 finalists. The average time of each player on court to reach the final was an hour and 14 minutes in Mauresmo's case; an hour and nine in Henin-Hardenne's. But a short final was not on the cards, not when the opening game of the match included ten points – though most of them were fought out around the net – three of them break points to the Belgian, on which she eventually capitalised. Henin-Hardenne was taking the initiative from the off, rushing Mauresmo into errors, even volleying behind her serve on a couple of occasions. After 31 minutes, she had accounted for the first set.

Then, Mauresmo held to love in the first game of the second set and let out a roar. Not everyone heard it but Henin-Hardenne surely did for the Belgian began to mishit. At times there were more skied shots from her racket than your everyday Twenty-20 cricket match and once she struck a serve that almost hit her on the toe. Mauresmo took a 3-0 lead, but the crux of the match came midway through the second set when Henin-Hardenne broke back for 3-4, only to lose her service immediately to a forehand cross court which had the 2001 finalist thudding her racket into the turf.

Seeing that Henin-Hardenne was seized by doubts, Mauresmo moved in but even then she had to survive three break points when serving for the set, the third of which, a complete backhand return mishit on a second serve, began to sum up Henin-Hardenne's increasing frustrations. An ace from the French woman brought the final level.

Mauresmo's blocked returns of serve had begun to pay enormous dividends, so much so that she reached break point in the third game of the final set, prompting Henin-Hardenne to miss badly with an attempted crosscourt backhand. How would Mauresmo cope with the lead? Would she falter? Not a bit of it – the No.1 dropped a mere three points on her following three service games (Henin-Hardenne had to save another break point with a lunging forehand volley to prevent herself trailing 4-1). And so to 5-4. ➢

Mike Bryan and Bob Bryan

"As I walked back I could hear this huge crowd yelling and clapping and then, as I prepared to serve, there was complete silence," Mauresmo would say later. "I felt a little bit scared, a little bit alone. I missed a ball toss (her first of the final) because the wind picked up, and I knew the crowd were thinking what I was thinking." She served a couple of aces, both to the deuce court and reached match point. Second serve. The ball barely crawled over the net, a rally ensued and Henin-Hardenne netted a forehand. Would Mauresmo have ever been able to conjure a winner? We will never know.

Henin-Hardenne's reaction to her loss was not one of her finest. This was surely better than having to quit on the stool as she had in Melbourne, but there was no kiss on either cheek as was her wont when she won. Her handshake was woeful. And, at the prize-giving later, the only two people in the players' box who did not rise to their feet were Pierre-Yves, Justine's husband and Carlos Rodrigues, her coach. This was baffling and, it has to be said, rather lacking in respect. Henin-Hardenne walked behind the guard of honour of the ballkids, Mauresmo strode through the middle of their proud ranks.

All the tension gone from the afternoon, it was

Mike Bryan and Bob Bryan celebrate winning the Gentlemen's Doubles Final against Fabrice Santoro and Nenad Zimonjic

QUOTE of the Day

Q: Would you give me a one word association for The Championships you have won in order?
First, the French.
A: Gritty.
Q: The Australian?
A: Hot
Q: The US Open?
A: Loud.
Q: Wimbledon?
A: Special.
MIKE BRYAN, OF THE WINNING BRYAN BROTHERS TEAM.

time for Bob and Mike Bryan to lighten the load as only these two breast-beating Californians could. They had been thinking about the career slam in doubles for a while "going down with all the legends on that board," as Mike said. "When you meet people, they say 'have you won Wimbledon?' they don't say 'have you won the US Open?'" For an American, this was saying something.

Well, they hadn't won Wimbledon. Until now. Theirs was a fabulous victory, 6-3, 4-6, 6-4, 6-2 over Fabrice Santoro of France and Nenad Zimonjic of Serbian and Montenegro. It was full of the telephatic instincts that only twins could have, I suppose. They seemed to know each other's movement before they had figured out there own. No doubles pair crossed the net to such effect as the Bryans. Reflex points, as they termed them.

Fresh from lifting the doubles cup with his brother in the Royal Box, Bob was right back down on the court again, with Venus Williams in the final of the mixed against Andy Ram of Israel and Vera Zvonereva of Russia. Understandably, it was difficult for him to sustain the levels over another match and it was the ninth seeds who would prevail. But credit to Venus, who overcame her singles loss so early, stuck around and played another final. Not bad for a team that only settled on being a team a day before The Championships. ●

Bob Bryan and Venus Williams

Vera Zvonareva and Andy Ram

135

FINAL Day
9.07.2006

FEDERER
VS
NADAL

Six players had won the Wimbledon men's singles title four times in succession, only two of them in short trousers. You had to return to the late Victorian era and the period immediately before the First World War, when The Championships were staged at Worple Road for the dominant periods of William Renshaw, Reggie and Laurie Doherty and the dashing Anthony Wilding, from Christchurch, New Zealand.

In 1913, the last year Wilding wooed the crowds with victory at Wimbledon – he was beaten in the 1914 final by Norman Brookes of Australia, enlisted and was killed in action in Neuve Chapelle, France in 1915 – "near perfect weather assisted in attracting record crowds, who each day packed the grounds to suffocation. Around 10,000 people were present at the ground on the second Friday when tickets for the Gentlemen's Challenge Round changed hands for £7 10/-."

By the late 1970s, it was Bjorn Borg of Swede who reigned surpreme, not only in London but Paris, too; and by the time we reached the 21st Century, Pete Sampras of the United States was running riot on the grass, en route to 14 grand slam singles trophies.

Roger Federer entered The 2006 Championships on the back of three successive titles and having just extended his grass court winning streak to 41 matches, equalling Borg's record. His opponent in the final was Rafael Nadal of Spain, who had won 60 consecutive matches on clay,

Anticipation

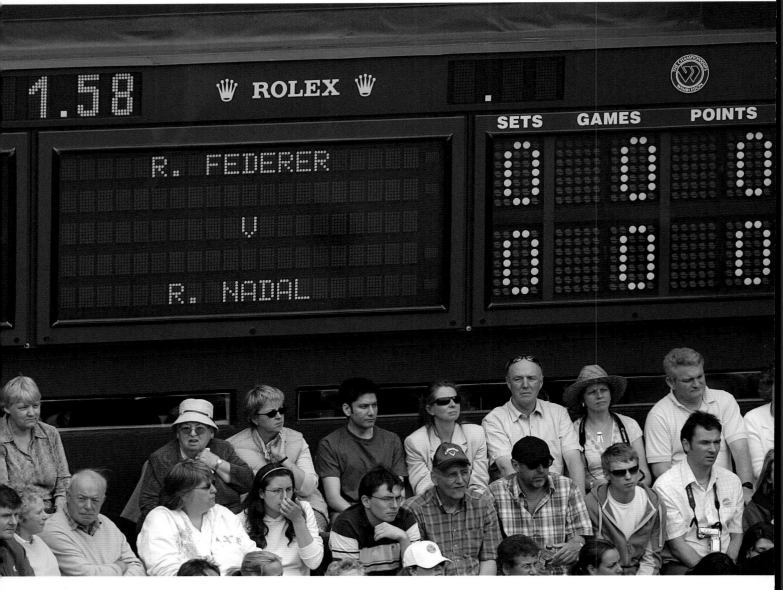

This is a special sensation. We are in the cathedral of tennis, so it is nice. I never think when I was young I could be in the final of Wimbledon. It was my dream but I never thought I could make it. So now I arrive today, I hope more years I can come back.

RAFAEL NADAL

reaching a crescendo in the final of the French Open, when Federer was his victim. Something would have to give. It could not have been a better climax to The Championships.

It was not a picture perfect day, there was scattered cloud and a fresh westerly wind had set in. When Nadal had come to the grounds on Saturday for his last practice session before the final, the enormity of what he had achieved had begun to sink in. He cried a little to himself – to think, a Spaniard who had set his heart on winning Wimbledon one day had made it through to the final. And not just that – this was a man who, six months earlier, had wondered whether he would play serious tennis again, such were the problems with his left foot. He didn't know the full extent of the injury, he had been in

tears at home over Christmas and, even when he flew to the United States in January for a fitting with special shoes, he could not know how his feet would react.

He came back to the tour in Marseille in February, making his way slowly and gingerly around the court. There was no lingering pain and, within a couple of weeks, he was in Dubai, winning the title, beating Federer in the final. He would do so again in Monte Carlo, Rome and Paris. On the back of his left shoe was stencilled 'Vamos' and on the right 'Rafa'. He was living up to that exhortation. But he remembered when times were bleak.

Federer had dropped only 52 games in reaching the final, the fewest in the Open Era. Whatever happened to him in the recent past, when faced with the presence and pulsating game of Nadal, ➤

Rafael Nadal

Roger Federer

could surely not happen at Wimbledon, irrespective of the 20 year-old's apparent hold.

When the first set disappeared in 24 minutes, Nadal having won 12 points and no games, Federer had stepped up emphatically.

But, as in the French Open final, having won the first set, Federer paused for breath and Nadal seized his chance. The 20 year-old leapt in the air when he reached 15-all in the first game of the second set, and broke the Champion by inducing a forehand mishit. The final was now a match. Nadal had begun to serve with such precision and variations of pace that it seemed sure he would take the set but, serving for it, he in turn was undone by those vagaries of bounce that a grass court, having had two week's wear, can contrive.

Serving at 5-4, he suddenly had to stoop forward to play a mid-court forehand cross-court and nudged it wide, double-faulted and then mistimed a forehand after Federer had caught him flat footed with a perfectly weighted service return. Even then, Nadal led 3-1 in the tie-break but the balance shifted when Federer conjured a remarkable forehand 'get', to force Nadal into a forehand error, immediately followed by a second, from mid court. On his third set point, Federer's deep second serve was the conduit for him to extend his lead.

Would he become the first man since Bjorn Borg in 1980 and only the fifth of all time (joining the American trio, Chuck McKinley, Tony Trabert and Donald Budge) to win this great title without relinquishing a set? Nadal had struggled to come to terms with the precision of Federer's sliced backhand, the spins and subtleties of his serve but more than that just the commanding presence the Swiss offers on this court. There was a sense early in the third set that the ferocious noises, that back up so many of his shots, were beginning to fade.

The set, though, contained only a single break point – Federer saving it with a service winner in the sixth game – serves were being held with distinction and so another tie-break was called for. Nadal sneaked ahead, Federer pulled it back to 2-2 but then struck a poor backhand into the net, prompting Nadal to lash out on his next forehand return and then, glory of glories, win a volleying exchange.

Vamos!

At this, the wind begn to pick up, swirls of dust formed as if we were back in Paris, eyebrows were raised among the intelligensia. Was Federer on the verge of being suckered again? But this was Wimbledon and such things did not happen here. The first three games of set four were edgy affairs and then Nadal had a rush of blood. From 30-0 up in the fourth game, he over-cooked a couple of forehands and then rushed in on break point, sending an attempted forehand smash first bounce into the backcourt canvas. Federer served ➤

for the match at 5-1 and played a couple of terrible forehands. Rome revisited. Nadal broke him and then held comprehensively. Federer stepped up again.

"Four points to go, Roger," a little boy shouted. Four was all he needed.

As they passed on the Centre Court circular, Federer, holding the gold cup by one handle and Nadal, a rim of the runners-up silver platter, brushed hands as if they were doubles partners who had just combined with a flourish. It was a gesture that spoke of the mutual respect and admiration that is the quintessence of their rivalry. It was a gesture that was the real spirit of Wimbledon.

Not only were these two men head and shoulders above the rest of the sport, they were the epitome of decency and fair play. So different in make up and personality but in what represents superstar quality, so much the same. Federer's 6-0, 7-6, 6-7, 6-3 victory in two hours and 58 minutes was greeted in the manner it ought to by the player who'd lost it, having stretched every sinew not to lose.

"Maybe the first set was tough for me because Roger is playing different than the other guys," Nadal said. "He play with more slice, he change a lot the game and when he break me in the first game, then it's tough for me. I don't see very well the goal in the game, not very well the strategy. It

Boys' doubles champions: Kellen Damico and Nathaniel Schnugg

was tough to get to his level.

"I cannot see where he serves, he can change to some very good angles.

"He can serve here and he can serve there. That's tough, especially on this surface because it's faster, no? But I want to improve because I want to win here. On clay, on hard courts, here, we can improve.

Federer is difficult, but always we can improve."

Wimbledon then fell under the Yan/Zheng spell when China celebrated its first triumph on these famed old lawns. Zi Yan and Jie Zheng , having broken through in the Australian Open, came of age and aged everyone in the process. The pair required seven match points to win the ladies'

The Russian pair, Alisa Kleybanova and Anastasia Pavlyuchenkova defeat top seeds, Kristina Antoniychuk of the Ukraine and Alexandra Dulgheru of Romania in the Girls' doubles final

doubles title. Finally, at the conclusion of interminable rallies that often involved only one player from each side, Yan put away a forehand volley into the open court, for the blossoming Chinese pair to defeat Virginia Ruano Pascual and Paola Suarez, of Spain and Argentina, the far more experienced team, 6-3, 2-6, 6-2.

Bit by bit, Chinese tennis comes to the fore. The surge of attention that followed their success in Melbourne took its toll, for Yan and Zheng reached only one final in their next six events, but once they turned the corner, they accelerated away, winning 21 of 22 matches, culminating in the greatest moment of their careers. An illustration of their strength is that, in their third round and quarter final matches, they won the final set 6-0. In the final, too, it was their toughness in the latter stages of the match that made the difference against the 2004 champions.

It was not the end of the winning and the losing, though. Thiemo De Bakker from the Netherlands became the Boys' singles champion – a title previously won by such notables as Pat Cash, Stefan Edberg, Ivan Lendl and Roger Federer – defeating Marcin Gawron, a Polish qualifier, 6-2, 7-6; while Caroline Wozniacki, the fourth seed from Denmark, lifted the Girls' crown with a 3-6, 6-1, 6-3 victory over Magdalena Rybarikova from Slovakia.

If the Americans were more than a touch muted about their performances in the main events, there was pretty considerable consolation in the victory in the Boys' doubles for the unseeded Kellen Damico and Nathaniel Schnugg, who followed up their success in the first round over the No.1 seeds, by taking out the No.2 seeded pair, Martin Klizan and Andrei Martin of Slovakia, 7-6, 6-2 in the final.

Not surprisingly, at the Champions' Dinner at the Savoy Hotel, Tim Phillips, the Chairman of the Club, made one stumble during the presentations. You try pronouncing Alisa Kleybanova and Anastasia Pavlyuchenkova, without a minor tongue trip. The Russian pair won the Girls' doubles, defeating the top seeds, Kristina Antoniychuk of the Ukraine and Alexandra Dulgheru of Romania 6-1, 6-2.

The Woodies returned their names to the champions' roster in the 35-and-over Gentlemen's Invitational Doubles (they weren't, were they?) beating T.J. Middleton and David Wheaton of the USA 6-7, 7-5, 7-6. The men's over-45 title went to the South Africans, Johan Kriek and Kevin Curren who, in a repeat of the 2005 final, prevented an Aussie oldie whitewash, with a 7-5, 6-7, 7-6 win over the Macs, Paul McNamee and Peter McNamara.

The "Woodies"

The Ladies' 35 and over Invitational Doubles was won by Ros Nideffer (nee Fairbank), of South Africa and Jana Novotna, of the Czech Republic, who defeated Tracy Austin, of the USA and Nathalie Tauziat, of France, 6-4, 6-3.

And last, but by no means least, if the crowds that flocked to their event were a true barometer of its ever-increasing popularity, the Wheelchair Men's Doubles title went to exuberant Shingo Kunieda and Satoshi Saida, of Japan, who beat Michael Jeremiasz, of France – the 2006 ITF World champion – and Great Britain's Jayant Mistry 7-5, 6-2. ●

Roger Federer
The Gentlemen's Singles Championship

Amelie Mauresmo
The Ladies' Singles Championship

Bob Bryan & Michael Bryan
The Gentlemen's Doubles Championship

Zi Yan & Jie Zheng
The Ladies' Doubles Championship

Andy Ram & Vera Zvonareva
The Mixed Doubles Championship

Shingo Kunieda & Satoshi Saida
The Wheelchair Gentlemen's Doubles Championship

Alisa Kleybanova &
Anastasia Pavlyuchenkova
The Girls' Doubles Championship

Kellen Damico &
Nathaniel Schnugg
The Boys' Doubles Championship

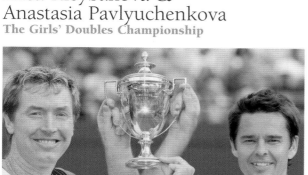

Todd Woodbridge & Mark Woodforde
The 35 & Over Gentlemen's Doubles Championship

Ros Nideffer & Jana Novotna
The 35 & Over Ladies' Doubles Championship

Caroline Wozniacki
The Girls' Singles Championship

Thiemo De Bakker
The Boys' Singles Championship

CHAMPIONSHIP
RECORDS
2006

EVENT I – THE GENTLEMEN'S SINGLES CHAMPIONSHIP 2006
HOLDER: R. FEDERER

The Winner became the holder, for the year only, of the CHALLENGE CUP presented by The All England Lawn Tennis and Croquet Club in 1887. The Winner received a silver replica of the Challenge Cup. A Silver Salver was presented to the Runner-up and a Bronze Medal to each defeated Semi-finalist. The matches were the best of five sets.

First Round

1. Federer, Roger [1] *(1)* (SUI)
2. Gasquet, Richard *(50)* (FRA)
3. Soderling, Robin *(37)* (SWE)
4. Henman, Tim *(64)* (GBR)
5. Mahut, Nicolas *(77)* (FRA)
6. Melzer, Jurgen *(78)* (AUT)
7. Novak, Jiri *(49)* (CZE)
8. Vliegen, Kristof [30] *(34)* (BEL)
9. Haas, Tommy [19] *(24)* (GER)
10. Vanek, Jiri *(92)* (CZE)
(WC) 11. Berlocq, Carlos *(89)* (ARG)
(Q) 12. Bloomfield, Richard *(259)* (GBR)
13. Arthurs, Wayne *(187)* (AUS)
14. Santoro, Fabrice *(45)* (FRA)
15. Hernych, Jan *(93)* (CZE)
16. Berdych, Tomas [13] *(14)* (CZE)
17. Robredo, Tommy [11] *(8)* (ESP)
18. Greul, Simon *(85)* (GER)
19. Goldstein, Paul *(65)* (USA)
20. Djokovic, Novak *(39)* (SCG)
21. Starace, Potito *(76)* (ITA)
22. Youzhny, Mikhail *(41)* (RUS)
23. Kunitsyn, Igor *(105)* (RUS)
24. Monfils, Gael [21] *(23)* (FRA)
25. Srichaphan, Paradorn [29] *(38)* (THA)
26. Calleri, Agustin *(58)* (ARG)
27. Karlovic, Ivo *(60)* (CRO)
28. Wawrinka, Stanislas *(67)* (SUI)
29. Sanguinetti, Davide *(69)* (ITA)
(Q) 30. Kim, Kevin *(108)* (USA)
31. Almagro, Nicolas *(47)* (ESP)
32. Ancic, Mario [7] *(10)* (CRO)
33. Nalbandian, David [4] *(3)* (ARG)
34. Moodie, Wesley *(73)* (RSA)
35. Portas, Albert *(115)* (ESP)
36. Clement, Arnaud *(57)* (FRA)
(Q) 37. Becker, Benjamin *(161)* (GER)
38. Chela, Juan Ignacio *(48)* (ARG)
39. Spadea, Vincent *(75)* (USA)
40. Verdasco, Fernando [28] *(30)* (ESP)
41. Ferrero, Juan Carlos [24] *(28)* (ESP)
42. Vicente, Fernando *(100)* (ESP)
(Q) 43. Karanusic, Roko *(163)* (CRO)
44. Schuettler, Rainer *(82)* (GER)
45. Malisse, Xavier *(43)* (BEL)
(Q) 46. Dorsch, Benedikt *(181)* (GER)
(Q) 47. Dancevic, Frank *(125)* (CAN)
48. Stepanek, Radek [14] *(13)* (CZE)
49. Johansson, Thomas [12] *(21)* (SWE)
50. Bjorkman, Jonas *(59)* (SWE)
51. Serra, Florent *(36)* (FRA)
52. Dlouhy, Lukas *(84)* (CZE)
(Q) 53. Galvani, Stefano *(141)* (ITA)
54. Waske, Alexander *(90)* (GER)
55. Bracciali, Daniele *(54)* (ITA)
56. Hrbaty, Dominik [20] *(22)* (SVK)
57. Mathieu, Paul-Henri [32] *(35)* (FRA)
(WC) 58. Philippoussis, Mark *(210)* (AUS)
59. Mirnyi, Max *(53)* (BLR)
60. Ramirez-Hidalgo, Ruben *(62)* (ESP)
61. Marach, Oliver *(96)* (AUT)
62. Wang, Yeu-Tzuoo *(99)* (TPE)
(Q) 63. Pless, Kristian *(139)* (DEN)
64. Blake, James [8] *(7)* (USA)
65. Hewitt, Lleyton [6] *(9)* (AUS)
66. Volandri, Filippo *(56)* (ITA)
67. Saretta, Flavio *(112)* (BRA)
68. Lee, Hyung-Taik *(102)* (KOR)
69. Montanes, Albert *(114)* (ESP)
70. Zib, Tomas *(126)* (CZE)
71. Muller, Gilles *(66)* (LUX)
72. Rochus, Olivier [26] *(29)* (BEL)
73. Ferrer, David [23] *(19)* (ESP)
(Q) 74. Stadler, Simon *(265)* (GER)
75. Minar, Ivo *(109)* (CZE)
76. Garcia-Lopez, Guillermo *(91)* (ESP)
77. Rusedski, Greg *(40)* (GBR)
78. Safin, Marat *(87)* (RUS)
79. Horna, Luis *(52)* (PER)
80. Gonzalez, Fernando [10] *(11)* (CHI)
81. Grosjean, Sebastien [15] *(26)* (FRA)
82. Simon, Gilles *(46)* (FRA)
(WC) 83. Delgado, Jamie *(447)* (GBR)
(Q) 84. Berrer, Michael *(116)* (GER)
(Q) 85. Granollers-Pujol, Marcel *(218)* (ESP)
(WC) 86. Pavel, Andrei *(79)* (ROM)
(WC) 87. Mackin, Alan *(367)* (GBR)
88. Baghdatis, Marcos [18] *(16)* (CYP)
89. Massu, Nicolas [31] *(33)* (CHI)
90. Murray, Andy *(44)* (GBR)
91. Phau, Bjorn *(61)* (GER)
92. Benneteau, Julien *(55)* (FRA)
93. Vik, Robin *(74)* (CZE)
94. Mayer, Florian *(63)* (GER)
95. Tipsarevic, Janko *(101)* (SCG)
96. Roddick, Andy [3] *(5)* (USA)
97. Ljubicic, Ivan [5] *(4)* (CRO)
98. Lopez, Feliciano *(49)* (ESP)
99. Gimelstob, Justin *(95)* (USA)
100. Rochus, Christophe *(70)* (BEL)
101. Di Mauro, Alessio *(83)* (ITA)
102. Martin, Alberto *(51)* (ESP)
103. Udomchoke, Danai *(97)* (THA)
104. Tursunov, Dmitry [27] *(31)* (RUS)
105. Nieminen, Jarkko [22] *(18)* (FIN)
106. Daniel, Marcos *(80)* (BRA)
107. Norman, Dick *(118)* (BEL)
(WC) 108. Lee, Martin *(252)* (GBR)
109. Sabau, Razvan *(131)* (ROM)
110. Kohlschreiber, Philipp *(88)* (GER)
(Q) 111. Falla, Alejandro *(127)* (COL)
112. Davydenko, Nikolay [9] *(6)* (RUS)
113. Gaudio, Gaston [16] *(12)* (ARG)
(LL) 114. Faurel, Jean-Christophe *(145)* (FRA)
(Q) 115. Peya, Alexander *(207)* (AUT)
(Q) 116. Labadze, Irakli *(166)* (GEO)
117. Van Gemerden, Melle *(106)* (NED)
(Q) 118. Goodall, Joshua *(398)* (GBR)
119. Fish, Mardy *(86)* (USA)
120. Ginepri, Robby [17] *(17)* (USA)
121. Agassi, Andre [25] *(20)* (USA)
122. Pashanski, Boris *(71)* (SCG)
123. Seppi, Andreas *(72)* (ITA)
(WC) 124. Baker, Jamie *(295)* (GBR)
125. Lu, Yen-Hsun *(119)* (TPE)
(Q) 126. Kendrick, Robert *(237)* (USA)
(WC) 127. Bogdanovic, Alex *(135)* (GBR)
128. Nadal, Rafael [2] *(2)* (ESP)

Second Round

- R.Federer [1] 6/3 6/2 6/2
- T.Henman 6/7(8) 6/3 6/2 1/6 6/3
- N.Mahut 6/7(3) 7/5 6/1 6/4
- K.Vliegen [30] 6/4 7/5 6/2
- T.Haas [19] 7/6(2) 7/5 6/4
- R.Bloomfield 6/2 6/2 6/2
- F.Santoro 7/6(3) 6/3 3/6 6/1
- T.Berdych [13] 6/3 6/4 7/5
- T.Robredo [11] 6/2 6/2 5/7 7/6(3)
- N.Djokovic 6/3 6/2 7/6(3)
- M.Youzhny 6/0 6/4 6/1
- I.Kunitsyn 5/7 7/6(7) 6/3 6/4
- A.Calleri 6/7(3) 7/5 6/3 3/6 6/3
- S.Wawrinka 7/6(5) 3/6 6/2 6/7(8) 11/9
- D.Sanguinetti 6/3 7/6(10) 6/1
- M.Ancic [7] 7/6(2) 7/5 7/6(4)
- D.Nalbandian [4] 6/3 6/4 6/1
- A.Clement 6/3 6/2 6/4
- B.Becker 6/3 3/6 6/3 6/4
- F.Verdasco [28] 3/6 6/4 7/6(1) 6/3
- J.C.Ferrero [24] 6/1 6/3 6/2
- R.Karanusic 7/6(7) 4/6 6/2 6/1
- X.Malisse 6/2 7/5 6/2
- R.Stepanek [14] 7/6(4) 6/4 6/4
- J.Bjorkman 3/6 7/6(4) 6/1 6/1
- L.Dlouhy 4/6 6/3 6/4 7/5
- S.Galvani 4/6 7/6(2) 6/4 3/6 16/14
- D.Bracciali 6/2 6/4 6/4
- M.Philippoussis 5/7 7/6(5) 6/3 7/6(12)
- M.Mirnyi 6/7(5) 6/4 6/3 6/3
- Y-T.Wang 6/1 7/6(2) 6/0
- J.Blake [8] 6/3 7/5 5/7 6/4
- L.Hewitt [6] 6/1 6/1 6/3
- H-T.Lee 7/6(10) 6/3 7/5
- T.Zib 6/3 6/4 7/6(7)
- O.Rochus [26] 6/4 7/5 6/3
- D.Ferrer [23] 6/1 6/4 6/4
- G.Garcia-Lopez 7/6(1) 4/6 7/6(3) 6/2
- M.Safin 6/4 6/4 6/4
- F.Gonzalez [10] 7/6(3) 7/5 6/2
- S.Grosjean [15] 6/4 6/2 6/4
- J.Delgado 6/4 6/2 3/6 3/6 6/3
- A.Pavel 7/6(4) 6/4 6/4
- M.Baghdatis [18] 6/4 6/7(4) 6/7(4) 7/5 6/2
- A.Murray 6/1 6/4 6/4
- J.Benneteau 5/7 6/4 6/2 7/6(6)
- F.Mayer 6/3 6/3 6/3
- A.Roddick [3] 6/7(5) 6/4 7/6(6) 6/2
- I.Ljubicic [5] 6/3 6/4 5/7 3/6 11/9
- J.Gimelstob 6/3 6/4 6/4
- A.Martin 6/3 6/4 6/1
- D.Tursunov [27] 6/1 6/4 6/2
- J.Nieminen [22] 6/2 6/4 7/5
- M.Lee 6/2 7/6(2) 7/6(4)
- P.Kohlschreiber 6/4 6/4 3/6 7/6(1)
- A.Falla 2/6 7/6(4) 7/6(8) 6/3
- G.Gaudio [16] 7/5 3/6 6/2 6/4
- I.Labadze 6/4 4/6 5/7 6/3 6/1
- M.Van Gemerden 6/4 7/5 7/5
- M.Fish 6/3 6/2 6/4
- A.Agassi [25] 2/6 6/2 6/4 6/3
- A.Seppi 6/3 6/7(3) 6/4 6/3
- R.Kendrick 7/6(5) 6/3 6/0
- R.Nadal [2] 6/4 7/6(3) 6/4

Third Round

- R.Federer [1] 6/4 6/0 6/2
- N.Mahut 6/4 6/4 6/3
- T.Haas [19] 6/3 6/4 7/6(4)
- T.Berdych [13] 6/4 6/7(6) 2/6 7/6(5) 6/4
- N.Djokovic 7/6(5) 6/2 6/4
- M.Youzhny 6/3 6/1 3/0 Ret'd
- S.Wawrinka 7/6(5) 7/5 6/3
- M.Ancic [7] 6/4 6/2 6/1
- D.Nalbandian [4] 6/4 6/4 6/3
- F.Verdasco [28] 6/4 6/7(7) 4/6 6/3 9/7
- J.C.Ferrero [24] 6/7(0) 6/3 6/4 6/4
- R.Stepanek [14] 6/3 6/7(4) 7/5 6/1
- J.Bjorkman 6/3 6/4 4/6 1/6 6/4
- D.Bracciali 6/3 6/7(3) 6/3 6/4
- M.Mirnyi 7/6(6) 6/4 6/7(5) 6/3
- J.Blake [8] 6/4 6/2 4/6 6/4
- L.Hewitt [6] 6/7(4) 6/2 7/6(6) 6/7(5) 6/4
- O.Rochus [26] 6/1 6/1 6/0
- D.Ferrer [23] 7/6(2) 7/5 6/3
- F.Gonzalez [10] 4/6 6/7(4) 6/4 6/4 6/4
- S.Grosjean [15] 6/3 6/2 6/4
- M.Baghdatis [18] 3/0 Ret'd
- A.Murray 7/6(5) 6/4 4/6 6/1
- A.Roddick [3] 6/4 6/1 6/2
- I.Ljubicic [5] 6/3 7/6(1) 7/5
- D.Tursunov [27] 6/1 7/5 6/4
- J.Nieminen [22] 6/4 6/0 6/3
- P.Kohlschreiber 6/4 6/4 3/6 7/6(4)
- I.Labadze 6/4 6/2 6/3
- M.Fish 6/2 6/0 6/1
- A.Agassi [25] 6/4 7/6(2) 6/4
- R.Nadal [2] 6/7(4) 3/6 7/6(2) 7/5 6/4

Fourth Round

- R.Federer [1] 6/3 7/6(2) 6/4
- T.Berdych [13] 2/6 7/5 7/6(7) 4/6 8/6
- N.Djokovic 4/6 6/2 6/3 6/3
- M.Ancic [7] 7/6(5) 7/5 6/3
- D.Nalbandian [4] 6/4 6/4 6/3
- R.Stepanek [14] 7/6(9) 7/6(9) 6/2
- J.Bjorkman 7/5 6/2 6/1
- L.Hewitt [6] 6/7(4) 6/2 7/6(6) 6/7(5) 6/4
- D.Ferrer [23] 4/6 2/6 6/2 6/3 6/4
- M.Baghdatis [18] 6/4 6/4 6/1
- A.Murray 7/6(4) 6/4 6/4
- D.Tursunov [27] 5/7 4/6 6/1 7/6(6) 6/2
- J.Nieminen [22] 1/6 6/3 7/6(4)
- I.Labadze 6/2 0/0 Ret'd
- R.Nadal [2] 6/3 7/6(4) 6/3

Quarter-Finals

- R.Federer [1] 6/3 6/3 6/4
- M.Ancic [7] 6/4 4/6 4/6 7/5 6/3
- R.Stepanek [14] 7/6(4) 6/4 6/4 6/2
- J.Bjorkman 6/3 7/6(6) 4/6 2/6 6/3
- M.Baghdatis [18] 6/3 6/4 7/6(2)
- A.Murray 7/6(4) 6/4 6/4
- J.Nieminen [22] 7/5 6/4 6/7(2) 6/7(6) 9/7
- R.Nadal [2] 6/3 7/6(4) 6/3

Semi-Finals

- R.Federer [1] 6/4 6/4 6/4
- J.Bjorkman 7/6(3) 4/6 6/7(5) 7/6(7) 6/4
- M.Baghdatis [18] 6/1 5/7 7/6(5) 6/2
- R.Nadal [2] 6/1 7/5 6/3

Final

- R.Federer [1] 6/2 6/0 6/2
- R.Nadal [2] 6/3 6/4 6/4

Winner

- R.Federer [1] 6/0 7/6(5) 6/7(2) 6/3

EVENT II – THE GENTLEMEN'S DOUBLES CHAMPIONSHIP 2006
HOLDERS: S. HUSS & W. MOODIE

The Winners became the holders, for the year only, of the CHALLENGE CUPS presented by the OXFORD UNIVERSITY LAWN TENNIS CLUB in 1884 and the late SIR HERBERT WILBERFORCE in 1937. The Winners received a silver replica of the Challenge Cup. A Silver Salver was presented to each of the Runners-up, and a Bronze Medal to each defeated Semi-finalist. The matches were the best of five sets.

First Round

1. B.Bryan (USA) & M.Bryan (USA) [1]
2. A.Delic (USA) & J.Kerr (AUS)
3. M.Mertinak (SVK) & P.Pala (CZE)
4. L.Azzaro (ITA) & A.Di Mauro (ITA)
(WC) 5. M.Lee (GBR) & J.Marray (GBR)
6. A.Fisher (AUS) & B.Reynolds (USA)
(LL) 7. F.Niemeyer (CAN) & G.Weiner (USA)
8. M.Bhupathi (IND) & A.Waske (GER) [13]
9. L.Dlouhy (CZE) & P.Vizner (CZE) [11]
10. J.Benneteau (FRA) & N.Mahut (FRA)
11. L.Burgsmuller (GER) & O.Marach (AUT)
12. D.Sanguinetti (ITA) & A.Seppi (ITA)
13. W.Arthurs (AUS) & J.Gimelstob (USA)
14. D.Ferrer (ESP) & T.Robredo (ESP)
15. I.Minar (CZE) & J.Vanek (CZE)
16. J.Erlich (ISR) & A.Ram (ISR) [5]
17. M.Knowles (BAH) & D.Nestor (CAN) [3]
18. L.Arnold (ARG) & D.Nalbandian (ARG)
19. P.Goldstein (USA) & J.Thomas (USA)
20. Y.Allegro (SUI) & K.Vliegen (BEL)
21. N.Almagro (ESP) & A.Portas (ESP)
22. P.Starace (ITA) & L.Zovko (CRO)
(WC) 23. J.Auckland (GBR) & J.Delgado (GBR)
24. W.Black (ZIM) & J.Coetzee (RSA) [14]
25. S.Huss (AUS) & W.Moodie (RSA) [9]
26. M.Daniel (BRA) & F.Vicente (ESP)
27. C.Kas (GER) & F.Mayer (GER)
28. A.Peya (AUT) & B.Phau (GER)
(Q) 29. K.Kim (USA) & C.Mamiit (PHI)
(LL) 30. S.Ratiwatana (THA) & S.Ratiwatana (THA)
(Q) 31. N.Bamford (GBR) & J.May (GBR)
32. S.Aspelin (SWE) & T.Perry (AUS) [8]
33. M.Damm (CZE) & L.Paes (IND) [7]
34. J.Tipsarevic (SCG) & M.Youzhny (RUS)
35. J.Hernych (CZE) & D.Skoch (CZE)
36. J.Nieminen (FIN) & G.Oliver (USA)
37. P.Petzschner (GER) & O.Rochus (BEL)
38. J.Levinsky (CZE) & R.Lindstedt (SWE)
39. C.Suk (CZE) & R.Vik (CZE)
40. F.Cermak (CZE) & L.Friedl (CZE) [12]
41. C.Haggard (RSA) & D.Hrbaty (SVK) [16]
42. T.Phillips (USA) & R.Wassen (NED)
43. A.Martin (ESP) & R.Ramirez-Hidalgo (ESP)
(Q) 44. I.Labadze (GEO) & D.Vemic (SCG)
45. T.Parrott (USA) & V.Spadea (USA)
46. M.Kohlmann (GER) & R.Schuettler (GER)
47. F.Serra (FRA) & G.Simon (FRA)
48. P.Hanley (AUS) & K.Ullyett (ZIM) [4]
49. F.Santoro (FRA) & N.Zimonjic (SCG) [6]
50. P.Kohlschreiber (GER) & D.Tursunov (RUS)
51. C.Rochus (BEL) & S.Wawrinka (SUI)
(WC) 52. J.Goodall (GBR) & R.Hutchins (GBR)
(LL) 53. Z.Fleishman (USA) & R.Smeets (AUS)
(WC) 54. C.Fleming (GBR) & J.Murray (GBR)
(Q) 55. R.Delgado (PAR) & A.Sa (BRA)
56. M.Fyrstenberg (POL) & M.Matkowski (POL) [10]
57. M.Garcia (ARG) & S.Prieto (ARG) [15]
58. I.Ljubicic (CRO) & U.Vico (ITA)
59. J.Melzer (AUT) & G.Muller (LUX)
60. D.Bracciali (ITA) & N.Djokovic (SCG)
(LL) 61. T.Cakl (CZE) & P.Snobel (CZE)
62. L.Kubot (POL) & T.Zib (CZE)
63. T.Cibulec (CZE) & J.Novak (CZE)
64. J.Bjorkman (SWE) & M.Mirnyi (BLR) [2]

Second Round

B.Bryan & M.Bryan [1]
6/7(2) 6/3 6/7(4) 6/3 11/9

M.Mertinak & P.Pala
6/3 6/2 6/3

A.Fisher & B.Reynolds
6/1 7/6(5) 6/4

F.Niemeyer & G.Weiner
7/6(2) 6/3 7/6(7)

L.Dlouhy & P.Vizner [11]
7/6(1) 6/4 3/6 6/3

L.Burgsmuller & O.Marach
5/7 4/6 6/3 6/4 6/4

W.Arthurs & J.Gimelstob
5/7 6/3 6/4 6/2

J.Erlich & A.Ram [5]
6/2 6/1 6/4

M.Knowles & D.Nestor [3]
4/6 6/3 6/4 6/2

Y.Allegro & K.Vliegen
6/2 6/3 6/3

P.Starace & L.Zovko
6/3 7/6(3) 6/3

J.Auckland & J.Delgado
6/4 4/6 2/6 6/4 6/3

S.Huss & W.Moodie [9]
6/2 6/1 6/7(1) 6/1

A.Peya & B.Phau
6/1 7/6(5) 6/4

S.Ratiwatana & S.Ratiwatana
6/4 3/6 6/3 6/7(5) 8/6

S.Aspelin & T.Perry [8]
6/4 6/3 6/3

M.Damm & L.Paes [7]
7/6(4) 6/3 0/0 Ret'd

J.Hernych & D.Skoch
3/6 6/3 7/6(1) 6/1

P.Petzschner & O.Rochus
6/4 6/2 3/6 6/3

C.Suk & R.Vik
7/5 6/7(10) 6/4 7/6(2)

T.Phillips & R.Wassen
6/4 3/6 4/6 6/3 6/4

I.Labadze & D.Vemic
6/3 2/6 7/5 6/2

M.Kohlmann & R.Schuettler
6/7(4) 6/4 6/4 6/7(2) 6/1

P.Hanley & K.Ullyett [4]
6/3 6/4 6/4

F.Santoro & N.Zimonjic [6]
7/6(3) 6/2 7/6(6)

J.Goodall & R.Hutchins
3/6 4/6 7/6(4) 6/4 6/3

Z.Fleishman & R.Smeets
7/6(6) 6/4 7/5

R.Delgado & A.Sa
2/6 6/4 6/3 4/6 6/3

M.Garcia & S.Prieto [15]
7/6(4) 6/3 6/4

D.Bracciali & N.Djokovic
7/6(5) 7/6(5) 7/6(3)

L.Kubot & T.Zib
6/3 6/4 6/3

J.Bjorkman & M.Mirnyi [2]
6/3 6/2 6/2

Third Round

B.Bryan & M.Bryan [1]
6/1 6/4 6/4

A.Fisher & B.Reynolds
3/6 6/3 6/2 6/2

L.Dlouhy & P.Vizner [11]
4/6 6/2 7/6(6) 7/6(4)

J.Erlich & A.Ram [5]
7/5 6/3 3/6 7/6(6)

M.Knowles & D.Nestor [3]
6/4 4/6 7/6(8) 6/2

J.Auckland & J.Delgado
7/6(4) 6/1 7/5

S.Huss & W.Moodie [9]
7/5 6/7(4) 3/6 7/5 6/3

S.Aspelin & T.Perry [8]
6/4 6/4 6/2

M.Damm & L.Paes [7]
6/4 6/4 6/3

C.Suk & R.Vik
4/6 6/3 6/4 6/2

I.Labadze & D.Vemic
4/6 4/6 6/3 7/5 6/4

P.Hanley & K.Ullyett [4]
6/4 7/6(1) 6/7(5) 7/6(5)

F.Santoro & N.Zimonjic [6]
6/7(3) 6/4 6/4 6/4

R.Delgado & A.Sa
6/2 6/3 6/2

M.Garcia & S.Prieto [15]
6/4 7/6(3) 6/4

J.Bjorkman & M.Mirnyi [2]
6/3 6/2 6/2

Quarter-Finals

B.Bryan & M.Bryan [1]
6/7(5) 6/4 6/4 6/2

L.Dlouhy & P.Vizner [11]
7/6(4) 6/4 4/6 7/6(5)

M.Knowles & D.Nestor [3]
7/6(3) 6/4 7/5

S.Aspelin & T.Perry [8]
6/7(5) 7/5 7/6(5) 7/6(4)

M.Damm & L.Paes [7]
6/2 6/1 7/6(1)

P.Hanley & K.Ullyett [4]
6/3 6/7(5) 6/3 6/7(4) 9/7

F.Santoro & N.Zimonjic [6]
6/4 6/4 7/6(7)

J.Bjorkman & M.Mirnyi [2]
6/1 6/4 6/7(4) 6/3

Semi-Finals

B.Bryan & M.Bryan [1]
7/6(4) 7/6(5) 6/1

M.Knowles & D.Nestor [3]
5/7 6/3 6/7(5) 6/3 23/21

M.Damm & L.Paes [7]
7/6(8) 6/7(5) 6/7(5) 7/6(7) 6/2

F.Santoro & N.Zimonjic [6]
6/2 6/1 7/5

Final

B.Bryan & M.Bryan [1]
6/4 6/7(3) 7/6(3) 6/1

F.Santoro & N.Zimonjic [6]

Winners

B.Bryan & M.Bryan [1]
6/3 4/6 6/4 6/2

Heavy type denotes seeded players. The figure in brackets against names denotes the order in which they have been seeded. (WC)=Wild card. (Q)=Qualifier. (LL)=Lucky loser.

EVENT III – THE LADIES' SINGLES CHAMPIONSHIP 2006
HOLDER: MISS V. WILLIAMS

The Winner became the holder, for the year only, of the CHALLENGE TROPHY presented by The All England Lawn Tennis and Croquet Club in 1886. The Winner received a silver replica of the Trophy. A Silver Salver was presented to the Runner-up and a Bronze Medal to each defeated Semi-finalist. The matches were the best of three sets.

	First Round	Second Round	Third Round	Fourth Round	Quarter-Finals	Semi-Finals	Final
(Q)	1. **Mauresmo, Amelie [1]** *(1)* (FRA) 2. Abramovic, Ivana *(192)* (CRO)	Miss A.Mauresmo [1] 6/0 6/0	Miss A.Mauresmo [1] 6/4 6/2	Miss A.Mauresmo [1] 6/1 6/2	Miss A.Mauresmo [1] 6/3 6/4	Miss A.Mauresmo [1] 6/1 3/6 6/3	Miss A.Mauresmo [1] 6/3 3/6 6/2
	3. Krajicek, Michaella *(39)* (NED) 4. Stosur, Samantha *(50)* (AUS)	Miss S.Stosur 7/5 6/3					
	5. Gajdosova, Jarmila *(86)* (SVK)	Miss N.J.Pratt 6/2 6/3	Miss N.J.Pratt 2/6 6/4 6/4				
(Q)	6. Pratt, Nicole *(136)* (AUS) 7. Diaz-Oliva, Mariana *(93)* (ARG)						
	8. **Golovin, Tatiana [29]** *(33)* (FRA)	Miss T.Golovin [29] 3/6 6/2 9/7					
	9. **Ivanovic, Ana [19]** *(22)* (SCG) 10. Gagliardi, Emmanuelle *(119)* (SUI)	Miss A.Ivanovic [19] 7/5 7/6(4)	Miss A.Ivanovic [19] 6/1 6/2	Miss A.Ivanovic [19] 3/6 7/6(3) 6/1			
(WC)	11. Domachowska, Marta *(66)* (POL) 12. Borwell, Sarah *(249)* (GBR)	Miss S.Borwell 6/7(3) 6/4					
	13. Washington, Mashona *(120)* (USA) 14. Schruff, Julia *(61)* (GER)	Miss M.Washington 6/3 6/4	Miss D.Safina [14] 4/6 6/4 6/1				
	15. Craybas, Jill *(43)* (USA) 16. **Safina, Dinara [14]** *(17)* (RUS)	Miss D.Safina [14] 3/6 7/5 7/5					
	17. **Myskina, Anastasia [9]** *(11)* (RUS)	Miss A.Myskina [9] 6/0 6/4	Miss A.Myskina [9] 6/2 6/1	Miss A.Myskina [9] 6/3 6/4	Miss A.Myskina [9] 6/4 7/6(5)		
(WC)	18. Black, Cara *(225)* (ZIM) 19. Muller, Martina *(74)* (GER)	Miss M.Muller 6/4 6/4					
	20. Kanepi, Kaia *(70)* (EST)						
(Q)	21. Fernandez, Clarisa *(198)* (ARG) 22. Martinez Granados, Concepcion *(92)* (ESP)	Miss C.Fernandez 6/2 4/6 4/3 Ret'd	Miss A.Medina Garrigues [23] 6/7(7) 7/5 11/9				
	23. Hsieh, Su-Wei *(126)* (TPE) 24. **Medina Garrigues, Anabel [23]** *(27)* (ESP)	Miss A.Medina Garrigues [23] 6/3 6/2					
	25. **Jankovic, Jelena [26]** *(29)* (SCG)	Miss J.Jankovic [26] 6/3 6/4	Miss J.Jankovic [26] 6/2 4/6 6/4	Miss J.Jankovic [26] 7/6(8) 4/6 6/4			
(LL)	26. Dominguez-Lino, Lourdes *(48)* (ESP) 27. Vakulenko, Julia *(90)* (UKR)	Miss V.King 5/4 Ret'd					
	28. King, Vania *(88)* (USA) 29. Raymond, Lisa *(84)* (USA)	Miss L.M.Raymond 3/5 Ret'd	Miss V.Williams [6] 6/7(4) 7/5 6/2				
	30. Shvedova, Yaroslava *(154)* (RUS) 31. Mattek, Bethanie *(103)* (USA)	Miss V.Williams [6] 6/1 6/0					
	32. **Williams, Venus [6]** *(12)* (USA) 33. **Sharapova, Maria [4]** *(4)* (RUS)	Miss M.Sharapova [4] 6/2 6/0	Miss M.Sharapova [4] 6/2 6/2	Miss M.Sharapova [4] 6/3 6/2	Miss M.Sharapova [4] 7/6(5) 3/6 6/3	Miss M.Sharapova [4] 6/1 6/4	
	34. Smashnova, Anna *(42)* (ISR) 35. Harkleroad, Ashley *(76)* (USA)	Miss A.Harkleroad 6/3 6/2					
	36. Kostanic, Jelena *(53)* (CRO) 37. Pous Tio, Laura *(94)* (ESP)	Miss M.Czink 6/3 6/1	Miss A.Frazier 6/2 6/3				
	38. Czink, Melinda *(77)* (HUN) 39. Frazier, Amy *(80)* (USA)	Miss A.Frazier 3/6 6/3 6/4					
	40. **Santangelo, Mara [32]** *(35)* (ITA) 41. **Peer, Shahar [20]** *(24)* (ISR)	Miss S.Peer [20] 6/2 6/1	Miss S.Peng 6/4 7/6(5)	Miss F.Pennetta [16] 6/2 6/4			
	42. Fedak, Yuliana *(78)* (UKR) 43. Daniilidou, Eleni *(52)* (GRE)	Miss S.Peng 6/4 6/4					
	44. Peng, Shuai *(46)* (CHN) 45. Ani, Maret *(72)* (EST)	Miss L.Granville 6/1 7/6(3)	Miss F.Pennetta [16] 6/2 6/1				
	46. Granville, Laura *(57)* (USA) 47. Kloesel, Sandra *(121)* (GER)	Miss F.Pennetta [16] 5/7 6/4 6/2					
	48. **Pennetta, Flavia [16]** *(19)* (ITA) 49. **Schiavone, Francesca [11]** *(14)* (ITA)	Miss M.South 6/3 6/4	Miss S.Perry 7/6(5) 6/2	Miss S.Perry 7/5 6/3			
(WC)	50. South, Melanie *(305)* (GBR) 51. Perry, Shenay *(62)* (USA)	Miss S.Perry 7/5 5/7 8/6					
(Q)	52. Barrois, Kristina *(156)* (GER) 53. Rodionova, Anastassia *(106)* (RUS)	Miss A.Rodionova 1/6 7/6(5) 6/4	Miss S.Bammer 6/4 6/4				
	54. Loit, Emilie *(51)* (FRA) 55. Bammer, Sybille *(47)* (AUT)	Miss S.Bammer 7/5 7/5					
	56. **Dechy, Nathalie [22]** *(23)* (FRA) 57. **Likhovtseva, Elena [25]** *(26)* (RUS)	Mrs E.Likhovtseva [25] 6/0 6/2	Mrs E.Likhovtseva [25]	Miss E.Dementieva [7] 7/5 6/4	Miss E.Dementieva [7] 6/2 6/0	Miss E.Dementieva [7] 6/2 6/0	
	58. Foretz, Stephanie *(85)* (FRA) 59. Sun, Tiantian *(100)* (CHN)	Miss T.Sun 6/3 6/4					
	60. Vierin, Nathalie *(112)* (ITA) 61. Shaughnessy, Meghann *(73)* (USA)	Miss M.Shaughnessy 4/6 6/2 6/3	Miss E.Dementieva [7] 5/7 6/4 7/5				
	62. Bondarenko, Alona *(54)* (UKR) 63. Mirza, Sania *(38)* (IND)	Miss E.Dementieva [7] 7/6(5) 7/5					
	64. **Dementieva, Elena [7]** *(8)* (RUS) 65. **Schnyder, Patty [8]** *(10)* (SUI)	Miss P.Schnyder [8] 2/6 7/6(4) 6/2	Mrs S.Bremond 4/6 6/1 6/4	Mrs S.Bremond 7/6(11) 6/3			
	66. Serra Zanetti, Antonella *(98)* (ITA) 67. Yakimova, Anastasiya *(55)* (BLR)	Mrs S.Bremond 7/5 6/3					
(Q)	68. Bremond, Severine *(129)* (FRA) 69. Sromova, Hana *(87)* (CZE)	Miss V.Ruano Pascual 6/4 6/3	Miss G.Dulko [31] 7/5 6/4				
	70. Ruano Pascual, Virginia *(91)* (ESP) 71. Laine, Emma *(67)* (FIN)						
	72. **Dulko, Gisela [31]** *(31)* (ARG)	Miss G.Dulko [31] 7/6(11) 6/1					
	73. **Sugiyama, Ai [18]** *(21)* (JPN)	Miss A.Sugiyama [18] 6/4 7/5	Miss A.Sugiyama [18] 6/2 7/5	Miss A.Sugiyama [18] 7/5 3/6 6/4	Mrs S.Bremond 7/6(11) 6/3		
(WC)	74. Cavaday, Naomi *(517)* (GBR) 75. Dushevina, Vera *(65)* (RUS)	Miss A.Morigami 1/6 6/4 6/2					
	76. Morigami, Akiko *(60)* (JPN) 77. Garbin, Tathiana *(68)* (ITA)	Miss T.Garbin 2/6 7/6(2) 6/2	Miss M.Hingis [12] 6/1 6/2				
(WC)	78. O'Brien, Katie *(235)* (GBR) 79. Savchuk, Olga *(102)* (UKR)	Miss M.Hingis [12] 6/2 6/2					
	80. **Hingis, Martina [12]** *(15)* (SUI) 81. **Hantuchova, Daniela [15]** *(18)* (SVK)	Miss D.Hantuchova [15] 6/4 4/6 6/1	Miss D.Hantuchova [15] 6/3 4/6 7/5	Miss D.Hantuchova [15] 6/4 7/6(2)			
	82. Camerin, Maria Elena *(56)* (ITA) 83. Flipkens, Kirsten *(130)* (BEL)	Miss J.Jackson 4/6 6/4 6/1					
(Q)	84. Jackson, Jamea *(58)* (USA) 85. Molik, Alicia *(260)* (AUS)	Miss A.Molik 7/5 6/1	Miss K.Srebotnik [21] 6/2 6/1				
(WC)	86. Chan, Yung-Jan *(178)* (TPE) 87. Sucha, Martina *(64)* (SVK)						
(Q)	88. **Srebotnik, Katarina [21]** *(25)* (SLO)	Miss K.Srebotnik [21] 6/4 6/1					
	89. **Chakvetadze, Anna [30]** *(34)* (RUS) 90. Yan, Zi *(79)* (CHN)	Miss A.Chakvetadze [30] 6/3 6/2	Miss A.Chakvetadze [30] 6/4 3/6 6/3	Mrs J.Henin-Hardenne [3] 6/2 6/3	Mrs J.Henin-Hardenne [3] 6/3 6/1	Mrs J.Henin-Hardenne [3] 6/4 6/4	Mrs J.Henin-Hardenne [3] 6/4 7/6(4)
	91. Sanchez Lorenzo, Maria *(75)* (ESP) 92. Vesnina, Elena *(63)* (RUS)	Miss E.Vesnina 2/6 6/4 6/3					
	93. Nakamura, Aiko *(59)* (JPN) 94. Bychkova, Ekaterina *(81)* (RUS)	Miss E.Bychkova 6/3 1/6 6/3	Mrs J.Henin-Hardenne [3] 6/1 6/4				
	95. Yuan, Meng *(99)* (CHN) 96. **Henin-Hardenne, Justine [3]** *(3)* (BEL)	Mrs J.Henin-Hardenne [3] 6/0 6/1					
	97. **Kuznetsova, Svetlana [5]** *(6)* (RUS)	Miss S.Kuznetsova [5] 6/3 6/2	Miss S.Kuznetsova [5] 4/6 6/1 6/4	Miss N.Li [27] 3/6 6/2 6/3			
(Q)	98. Oprandi, Romina *(82)* (ITA) 99. Peschke, Kveta *(41)* (CZE)	Mrs K.Peschke 6/3 6/0					
	100. Brandi, Kristina *(116)* (PUR) 101. Tu, Meilen *(105)* (USA)	Miss M.Tu 6/3 6/0	Miss N.Li [27] 6/2 6/4				
(Q)	102. Bardina, Vasilisa *(117)* (RUS) 103. Razzano, Virginie *(89)* (FRA)	Miss N.Li [27] 6/2 6/0					
(Q)	104. **Li, Na [27]** *(30)* (CHN) 105. **Bartoli, Marion [24]** *(28)* (FRA)	Miss M.Bartoli [24] 6/0 6/2	Miss K.Sprem 3/6 6/2 6/3	Miss N.Vaidisova [10] 7/5 7/5	Miss N.Li [27] 4/6 6/1 6/3		
	106. Pin, Camille *(97)* (FRA) 107. Sprem, Karolina *(69)* (CRO)	Miss K.Sprem 6/0 6/2					
(WC)	108. Keothavong, Anne *(143)* (GBR) 109. Lisjak, Ivana *(95)* (CRO)	Miss K.Bondarenko 6/4 7/5	Miss N.Vaidisova [10] 6/1 6/1				
	110. Bondarenko, Kateryna *(111)* (UKR) 111. Koukalova, Klara *(45)* (CZE)	Miss N.Vaidisova [10] 7/5 7/5					
	112. **Vaidisova, Nicole [10]** *(13)* (CZE) 113. **Groenefeld, Anna-Lena [13]** *(16)* (GER)	Miss T.Pironkova 6/3 6/1	Miss A.Radwanska 7/5 7/6(5)	Miss A.Radwanska 6/3 6/2			
(WC)	114. Pironkova, Tsvetana *(83)* (BUL) 115. Radwanska, Agnieszka *(217)* (POL)	Miss A.Radwanska 7/5 6/4					
	116. Azarenka, Viktoria *(101)* (BLR) 117. Castano, Catalina *(36)* (COL)	Miss T.Tanasugarn 6/7(2) 6/1 6/2	Miss T.Tanasugarn 6/3 7/5				
(Q)	118. Tanasugarn, Tamarine *(164)* (THA) 119. Asagoe, Shinobu *(110)* (JPN)	Miss S.Asagoe 6/2 7/6(1)					
	120. **Kirilenko, Maria [17]** *(20)* (RUS) 121. **Arvidsson, Sofia [28]** *(32)* (SWE)	Miss E.Birnerova 6/2 6/4	Miss J.Zheng 7/6(6) 5/7 6/3	Miss K.Clijsters [2] 6/3 6/2	Miss K.Clijsters [2] 6/2 6/2	Miss K.Clijsters [2] 6/4 7/5	
	122. Birnerova, Eva *(122)* (CZE) 123. Zheng, Jie *(37)* (CHN)	Miss J.Zheng 7/5 6/2					
	124. Benesova, Iveta *(49)* (CZE) 125. Kutuzova, Viktoriya *(96)* (UKR)	Miss V.Kutuzova 6/4 3/3 Ret'd	Miss K.Clijsters [2] w/o				
	126. Osterloh, Lilia *(109)* (USA) 127. Zvonareva, Vera *(44)* (RUS)						
	128. **Clijsters, Kim [2]** *(2)* (BEL)	Miss K.Clijsters [2] 7/5 6/3					

EVENT IV – THE LADIES' DOUBLES CHAMPIONSHIP 2006
HOLDERS: MISS C. BLACK & MRS L. HUBER

The Winners became the holders, for the year only, of the CHALLENGE CUPS presented by H.R.H. PRINCESS MARINA, DUCHESS OF KENT, the late President of The All England Lawn Tennis and Croquet Club in 1949 and The All England Lawn Tennis and Croquet Club in 2001. The Winners received a silver replica of the Challenge Cup. A Silver Salver was presented to each of the Runners-up and a Bronze Medal to each defeated Semi-finalist. The matches were the best of three sets.

First Round	Second Round	Third Round	Quarter-Finals	Semi-Finals	Final	Winner
1. Miss L.M.Raymond (USA) & Miss S.Stosur (AUS) [1]						
2. Miss A.Frazier (USA) & Miss A.Spears (USA)	Miss L.M.Raymond & Miss S.Stosur [1] 7/5 6/2					
3. Miss M.Domachowska (POL) & Miss M.Sucha (SVK)		Miss L.M.Raymond & Miss S.Stosur [1] 6/4 6/2				
4. Miss M.Drake (CAN) & Miss N.Vaidisova (CZE)	Miss M.Drake & Miss N.Vaidisova 6/4 6/4					
5. Miss V.Razzano (FRA) & Miss A.Smashnova (ISR)			Miss V.Ruano Pascual & Miss P.Suarez 6/4 6/4			
6. Miss V.Ruano Pascual (ESP) & Miss P.Suarez (ARG)	Miss V.Ruano Pascual & Miss P.Suarez 6/2 6/1					
7. Miss S.Arvidsson (SWE) & Miss M.Muller (GER)		Miss V.Ruano Pascual & Miss P.Suarez 6/4 6/1				
8. Miss M.Bartoli (FRA) & Miss S.Peer (ISR) [17]	Miss M.Bartoli & Miss S.Peer [17] 6/1 6/1					
9. Miss E.Daniilidou (GRE) & Miss A.Medina Garrigues (ESP) [10]				Miss V.Ruano Pascual & Miss P.Suarez 6/7(4) 6/3 9/7		
(LL) 10. Miss C-W.Chan (TPE) & Miss S-W.Hsieh (TPE)	Miss E.Daniilidou & Miss A.Medina Garrigues [10] 6/4 6/2					
11. Miss A.Rodionova (RUS) & Miss A.Vanc (ROM)		Miss E.Daniilidou & Miss A.Medina Garrigues [10] 6/2 5/7 6/4				
12. Miss A.Chakvetadze (RUS) & Miss E.Vesnina (RUS)	Miss A.Rodionova & Miss A.Vanc 6/3 6/4					
(WC) 13. Miss S.Borwell (GBR) & Miss J.O'Donoghue (GBR)			Miss E.Daniilidou & Miss A.Medina Garrigues [10] 6/4 7/6(3)			
14. Miss M.Jugic-Salkic (BIH) & Miss E.Laine (FIN)	Miss M.Jugic-Salkic & Miss E.Laine 7/6(4) 7/5					
15. Miss E.Gagliardi (SUI) & Miss M.Santangelo (ITA)		Miss M.Jugic-Salkic & Miss E.Laine 6/2 6/7(4) 6/4				
16. Miss S.Asagoe (JPN) & Miss K.Srebotnik (SLO) [6]	Miss E.Gagliardi & Miss M.Santangelo 7/6(2) 6/2					
17. Miss D.Hantuchova (SVK) & Miss A.Sugiyama (JPN) [3]					Miss V.Ruano Pascual & Miss P.Suarez 6/4 6/3	
18. Miss J.Gajdosova (SVK) & Miss A.Harkleroad (USA)	Miss J.Gajdosova & Miss A.Harkleroad 6/3 6/4					
19. Miss I.Benesova (CZE) & Miss B.Strycova (CZE)		Miss J.Gajdosova & Miss A.Harkleroad 7/5 6/4				
20. Miss G.Navratilova (CZE) & Miss M.Pastikova (CZE)	Miss I.Benesova & Miss B.Strycova 2/6 6/1 6/3					
(WC) 21. Miss K.O'Brien (GBR) & Miss M.South (GBR)			Miss Y.Fedak & Miss T.Perebiynis 6/1 6/1			
(Q) 22. Miss Y.Fedak (UKR) & Miss T.Perebiynis (UKR)	Miss Y.Fedak & Miss T.Perebiynis 6/4 6/4					
23. Miss M.Ani (EST) & Miss M.Tu (USA)		Miss Y.Fedak & Miss T.Perebiynis 4/6 6/4 6/2				
24. Miss N.Dechy (FRA) & Miss G.Dulko (ARG) [16]	Miss M.Ani & Miss M.Tu 6/4 1/6 6/3					
25. Miss S.Kuznetsova (RUS) & Miss A.Mauresmo (FRA) [12]				Miss Y.Fedak & Miss T.Perebiynis 6/7(3) 6/4 6/4		
26. Miss M.E.Salerni (ARG) & Mrs M.Vento-Kabchi (VEN)	Miss S.Kuznetsova & Miss A.Mauresmo [12] 4/6 6/2 6/0					
(WC) 27. Miss C.Curran (GBR) & Miss J.Jackson (USA)		Miss L.Hradecka & Miss H.Sromova w/o				
(Q) 28. Miss L.Hradecka (CZE) & Miss H.Sromova (CZE)	Miss L.Hradecka & Miss H.Sromova 7/6(5) 6/2					
29. Miss T.Poutchek (BLR) & Miss A.Yakimova (BLR)			Miss A-L.Groenefeld & Miss M.Shaughnessy [5] 6/4 7/5			
(LL) 30. Miss M.Diaz-Oliva (ARG) & Miss N.Grandin (RSA)	Miss M.Diaz-Oliva & Miss N.Grandin 6/2 6/3					
31. Miss L.Dekmeijere (LAT) & Miss K.Kanepi (EST)		Miss A-L.Groenefeld & Miss M.Shaughnessy [5] 6/2 7/6(5)				
32. Miss A-L.Groenefeld (GER) & Miss M.Shaughnessy (USA) [5]	Miss A-L.Groenefeld & Miss M.Shaughnessy [5] 6/2 6/2					
33. Mrs L.Huber (RSA) & Miss M.Navratilova (USA) [7]					Miss Z.Yan & Miss J.Zheng [4] 6/3 3/6 6/2	
34. Miss A.Bondarenko (UKR) & Miss K.Bondarenko (UKR)	Mrs L.Huber & Miss M.Navratilova [7] 6/3 6/1					
35. Miss J.Jankovic (SCG) & Miss T.Krizan (SLO)		Mrs L.Huber & Miss M.Navratilova [7] 6/4 3/6 6/4				
36. Miss A.Ivanovic (SCG) & Miss M.Kirilenko (RUS)	Miss J.Jankovic & Miss T.Krizan 6/3 6/4					
(WC) 37. Mrs A.Keen (GBR) & Miss K.Keothavong (GBR)			Mrs L.Huber & Miss M.Navratilova [7] 7/5 6/0			
38. Miss C.Gullickson (USA) & Miss B.Stewart (AUS)	Miss C.Gullickson & Miss B.Stewart 6/4 6/7(7) 6/3					
39. Miss S.Sfar (TUN) & Miss J.Woehr (GER)		Mrs E.Likhovtseva & Miss A.Myskina [11] 6/4 6/3				
40. Mrs E.Likhovtseva (RUS) & Miss A.Myskina (RUS) [11]	Mrs E.Likhovtseva & Miss A.Myskina [11] 6/3 6/4					
41. Miss E.Loit (FRA) & Miss N.J.Pratt (AUS) [14]				Miss Z.Yan & Miss J.Zheng [4] 4/6 6/4 6/0		
42. Miss M.E.Camerin (ITA) & Miss T.Garbin (ITA)	Miss M.E.Camerin & Miss T.Garbin 7/5 6/7(3) 6/3					
43. Miss L.Dominguez-Lino (ESP) & Miss M.Sanchez Lorenzo (ESP)		Miss M.E.Camerin & Miss T.Garbin 6/3 6/3				
44. Miss L.Granville (USA) & Miss S.Perry (USA)	Miss L.Dominguez-Lino & Miss M.Sanchez Lorenzo 6/3 7/6(1)					
45. Miss J.Craybas (USA) & Miss J.Kostanic (CRO)			Miss Z.Yan & Miss J.Zheng [4] 4/6 6/2 6/0			
46. Miss J.Husarova (SVK) & Miss V.Zvonareva (RUS)	Miss J.Husarova & Miss V.Zvonareva 6/1 6/2					
(LL) 47. Miss M.Czink (HUN) & Miss V.King (USA)		Miss Z.Yan & Miss J.Zheng [4] 6/0 7/6(4)				
48. Miss Z.Yan (CHN) & Miss J.Zheng (CHN) [4]	Miss Z.Yan & Miss J.Zheng [4] 6/3 6/1					
49. Miss E.Dementieva (RUS) & Miss F.Pennetta (ITA) [8]					Miss Z.Yan & Miss J.Zheng [4] 6/2 7/6(3)	
50. Miss S.Bammer (AUT) & Miss J.Schruff (GER)	Miss E.Dementieva & Miss F.Pennetta [8] 6/3 6/3					
51. Miss M.Krajicek (NED) & Miss S.Mirza (IND)		Miss E.Dementieva & Miss F.Pennetta [8] 6/4 6/2				
52. Miss S.Foretz (FRA) & Miss A.Serra Zanetti (ITA)	Miss M.Krajicek & Miss S.Mirza 6/3 4/6 6/2					
53. Miss V.Dushevina (RUS) & Miss G.Voskoboeva (RUS)			Mrs K.Peschke & Miss F.Schiavone [9] 7/5 6/2			
54. Miss A.Morigami (JPN) & Miss A.Nakamura (JPN)	Miss V.Dushevina & Miss G.Voskoboeva 7/6(4) 6/7(4) 8/6					
55. Miss Y.Beygelzimer (UKR) & Miss E.Birnerova (CZE)		Mrs K.Peschke & Miss F.Schiavone [9] 3/6 7/6(3) 6/1				
56. Mrs K.Peschke (CZE) & Miss F.Schiavone (ITA) [9]	Mrs K.Peschke & Miss F.Schiavone [9] 6/1 7/5					
57. Miss T.Li (CHN) & Miss T.Sun (CHN) [13]			Miss C.Black & Miss R.P.Stubbs [2] 6/3 6/4			
58. Miss B.Mattek (USA) & Miss M.Washington (USA)	Miss B.Mattek & Miss M.Washington 4/6 6/3 6/2					
(Q) 59. Miss S.Cohen Aloro (FRA) & Miss M.Martinez Sanchez (ESP)		Miss S.Cohen Aloro & Miss M.Martinez Sanchez 6/3 7/5				
(Q) 60. Miss L.Osterloh (USA) & Miss A.Rolle (USA)	Miss S.Cohen Aloro & Miss M.Martinez Sanchez 6/1 6/2					
61. Miss K.Koukalova (CZE) & Miss V.Uhlirova (CZE)				Miss C.Black & Miss R.P.Stubbs [2] 1/6 7/6(5) 6/2		
62. Miss N.Li (CHN) & Miss S.Peng (CHN)	Miss N.Li & Miss S.Peng 6/3 6/4					
(WC) 63. Miss R.Llewellyn (GBR) & Miss K.Paterson (GBR)		Miss C.Black & Miss R.P.Stubbs [2] w/o				
64. Miss C.Black (ZIM) & Miss R.P.Stubbs (AUS) [2]	Miss C.Black & Miss R.P.Stubbs [2] 6/1 6/3					

Semi-Finals: Miss V.Ruano Pascual & Miss P.Suarez 6/7(4) 6/3 9/7 ; Miss Y.Fedak & Miss T.Perebiynis 6/7(3) 6/4 6/4 ; Miss Z.Yan & Miss J.Zheng [4] 4/6 6/4 6/0 ; Miss C.Black & Miss R.P.Stubbs [2] 1/6 7/6(5) 6/2

Final: Miss V.Ruano Pascual & Miss P.Suarez 6/4 6/3 ; Miss Z.Yan & Miss J.Zheng [4] 6/2 7/6(3)

Winner: Miss Z.Yan & Miss J.Zheng [4] 6/3 3/6 6/2

Heavy type denotes seeded players. The figure in brackets against names denotes the order in which they were seeded. (WC)=Wild card. (Q)=Qualifier. (LL)=Lucky loser.

EVENT V – THE MIXED DOUBLES CHAMPIONSHIP 2006
HOLDERS: M. BHUPATHI & MISS M. PIERCE

The Winners became the holders, for the year only, of the CHALLENGE CUPS presented by members of the family of the late Mr. S. H. SMITH in 1949 and The All England Lawn Tennis and Croquet Club in 2001. The Winners received a silver replica of the Challenge Cup. A Silver Salver was presented to each of the Runners-up and a Bronze Medal to each defeated Semi-finalist. The matches were the best of three sets.

First Round

1. **J.Bjorkman** (SWE) **& Miss L.M.Raymond** (USA) **[1]**
2. Bye
(WC) 3. J.Auckland (GBR) & Miss C.Curran (GBR)
4. L.Arnold (ARG) & Miss F.Schiavone (ITA)
5. R.Lindstedt (SWE) & Miss S.Arvidsson (SWE)
(WC) 6. A.Murray (GBR) & Miss K.Flipkens (BEL)
7. Bye
8. **F.Cermak** (CZE) **& Miss A-L.Groenefeld** (GER) **[16]**
9. **A.Ram** (ISR) **& Miss V.Zvonareva** (RUS) **[9]**
10. Bye
11. J.Levinsky (CZE) & Miss A.Chakvetadze (RUS)
12. C.Haggard (RSA) & Miss E.Daniilidou (GRE)
13. J.Gimelstob (USA) & Miss M.Shaughnessy (USA)
14. M.Matkowski (POL) & Miss M.Domachowska (POL)
15. Bye
16. **M.Knowles** (BAH) **& Miss M.Navratilova** (USA) **[8]**
17. **W.Black** (ZIM) **& Miss C.Black** (ZIM) **[3]**
18. Bye
(WC) 19. W.Arthurs (AUS) & Miss A.Molik (AUS)
(A) 20. L.Dlouhy (CZE) & Miss E.Birnerova (CZE)
21. D.Skoch (CZE) & Miss A.Vanc (ROM)
22. F.Gonzalez (CHI) & Miss G.Dulko (ARG)
23. Bye
24. **M.Bryan** (USA) **& Miss C.Morariu** (USA) **[13]**
25. **M.Damm** (CZE) **& Mrs K.Peschke** (CZE) **[10]**
26. Bye
27. M.Fyrstenberg (POL) & Miss J.Craybas (USA)
28. J.Thomas (USA) & Miss A.Rodionova (RUS)
29. T.Parrott (USA) & Miss S.Peng (CHN)
30. R.Wassen (NED) & Miss M.Krajicek (NED)
31. Bye
32. **N.Zimonjic** (SCG) **& Miss K.Srebotnik** (SLO) **[7]**
33. **T.Perry** (AUS) **& Miss R.P.Stubbs** (AUS) **[6]**
34. Bye
35. J.Kerr (AUS) & Miss B.Stewart (AUS)
36. S.Aspelin (SWE) & Miss T.Sun (CHN)
37. B.Bryan (USA) & Miss V.Williams (USA)
38. J.Coetzee (RSA) & Miss A.Sugiyama (JPN)
39. Bye
40. **M.Bhupathi** (IND) **& Miss Z.Yan** (CHN) **[11]**
41. **J.Erlich** (ISR) **& Miss D.Safina** (RUS) **[14]**
42. Bye
43. S.Prieto (ARG) & Miss F.Pennetta (ITA)
(WC) 44. C.Suk (CZE) & Miss H.Sukova (CZE)
45. G.Oliver (USA) & Miss M.Tu (USA)
(WC) 46. P.Hanley (AUS) & Miss T.Perebiynis (UKR)
47. Bye
48. **L.Paes** (IND) **& Miss S.Stosur** (AUS) **[4]**
49. **D.Nestor** (CAN) **& Mrs E.Likhovtseva** (RUS) **[5]**
50. Bye
51. A.Fisher (AUS) & Miss N.J.Pratt (AUS)
52. M.Mertinak (SVK) & Miss M.Sucha (SVK)
53. P.Vizner (CZE) & Miss S.Mirza (IND)
54. F.Verdasco (ESP) & Miss A.Medina Garrigues (ESP)
55. Bye
56. **L.Friedl** (CZE) **& Mrs L.Huber** (RSA) **[12]**
57. **K.Ullyett** (ZIM) **& Miss S.Peer** (ISR) **[15]**
58. Bye
59. W.Moodie (RSA) & Miss V.Dushevina (RUS)
60. P.Pala (CZE) & Miss C.Castano (COL)
61. M.Garcia (ARG) & Miss M.Santangelo (ITA)
62. S.Huss (AUS) & Miss B.Mattek (USA)
63. Bye
64. **M.Mirnyi** (BLR) **& Miss J.Zheng** (CHN) **[2]**

Second Round

J.Bjorkman & Miss L.M.Raymond [1]

J.Auckland & Miss C.Curran 2/3 Ret'd

A.Murray & Miss K.Flipkens 6/3 6/4

F.Cermak & Miss A-L.Groenefeld [16]

A.Ram & Miss V.Zvonareva [9]

C.Haggard & Miss E.Daniilidou 6/4 7/6(9)

J.Gimelstob & Miss M.Shaughnessy 6/4 6/2

M.Knowles & Miss M.Navratilova [8]

W.Black & Miss C.Black [3]

L.Dlouhy & Miss E.Birnerova 3/6 7/6(5) 6/4

F.Gonzalez & Miss G.Dulko 2/6 6/1 6/0

M.Bryan & Miss C.Morariu [13]

M.Damm & Mrs K.Peschke [10]

M.Fyrstenberg & Miss J.Craybas 6/4 6/4

R.Wassen & Miss M.Krajicek 7/6(3) 7/6(5)

N.Zimonjic & Miss K.Srebotnik [7]

T.Perry & Miss R.P.Stubbs [6]

S.Aspelin & Miss T.Sun 6/4 6/1

B.Bryan & Miss V.Williams 6/3 6/3

M.Bhupathi & Miss Z.Yan [11]

J.Erlich & Miss D.Safina [14]

S.Prieto & Miss F.Pennetta 6/4 6/3

P.Hanley & Miss T.Perebiynis 6/2 7/6(5)

L.Paes & Miss S.Stosur [4]

D.Nestor & Mrs E.Likhovtseva [5]

A.Fisher & Miss N.J.Pratt 6/3 6/2

P.Vizner & Miss S.Mirza 6/2 7/5

L.Friedl & Mrs L.Huber [12]

K.Ullyett & Miss S.Peer [15]

W.Moodie & Miss V.Dushevina 6/4 6/4

S.Huss & Miss B.Mattek 6/4 6/3

M.Mirnyi & Miss J.Zheng [2]

Third Round

J.Bjorkman & Miss L.M.Raymond [1] 6/3 6/2

F.Cermak & Miss A-L.Groenefeld [16] 6/4 6/2

A.Ram & Miss V.Zvonareva [9] 6/4 2/6 6/4

M.Knowles & Miss M.Navratilova [8] 6/2 7/6(4)

W.Black & Miss C.Black [3] 6/2 6/1

M.Bryan & Miss C.Morariu [13] w/o

M.Damm & Mrs K.Peschke [10] 6/3 7/6(13)

N.Zimonjic & Miss K.Srebotnik [7] 6/4 6/4

T.Perry & Miss R.P.Stubbs [6] 4/6 7/6(3) 6/4

B.Bryan & Miss V.Williams 6/4 6/1

S.Prieto & Miss F.Pennetta 1/6 6/4 6/3

L.Paes & Miss S.Stosur [4] 4/6 6/3 12/10

D.Nestor & Mrs E.Likhovtseva [5] 6/1 6/1

P.Vizner & Miss S.Mirza 6/1 6/1

W.Moodie & Miss V.Dushevina 6/3 6/4

M.Mirnyi & Miss J.Zheng [2] 6/2 6/2

Quarter-Finals

F.Cermak & Miss A-L.Groenefeld [16] w/o

A.Ram & Miss V.Zvonareva [9] 7/5 6/1

W.Black & Miss C.Black [3] 6/2 6/4

N.Zimonjic & Miss K.Srebotnik [7] 7/6(10) 6/7(3) 6/4

B.Bryan & Miss V.Williams 7/6(4) 6/3

L.Paes & Miss S.Stosur [4] 6/3 6/2

D.Nestor & Mrs E.Likhovtseva [5] 6/3 5/7 6/2

M.Mirnyi & Miss J.Zheng [2] 6/4 6/7(5) 9/7

Semi-Finals

A.Ram & Miss V.Zvonareva [9] 6/3 6/4

W.Black & Miss C.Black [3] 6/7(4) 6/4 11/9

B.Bryan & Miss V.Williams 7/6(3) 6/3

M.Mirnyi & Miss J.Zheng [2] 6/2 6/3

Final

A.Ram & Miss V.Zvonareva [9] 6/3 7/6(5)

B.Bryan & Miss V.Williams 7/5 7/5

Winner

A.Ram & Miss V.Zvonareva [9] 6/3 6/2

Heavy type denotes seeded players. The figure in brackets against names denotes the order in which they were seeded. (WC)=Wild card. (A)=Alternates.

EVENT VI – THE 35 AND OVER GENTLEMEN'S INVITATION DOUBLES 2006
HOLDERS: E. FERREIRA & P. HAARHUIS

The Winners became the holders, for the year only, of a cup presented by The All England Lawn Tennis and Croquet Club. The Winners received miniature silver salvers. A silver medal was presented to each of the Runners-up.

GROUP A	T.A. Woodbridge (AUS) & M. Woodforde (AUS)	M.J. Bates (GBR) & C. Wilkinson (GBR)	L. Jensen (USA) & M. Jensen (USA)	P. Aldrich (RSA) & D. Visser (RSA)	WINS	LOSSES
T.A. Woodbridge (AUS) & M. Woodforde (AUS)		7/6(12) 7/6(2) W	7/5 6/2 W	6/4 6/3 W	3	0
M.J. Bates (GBR) & C. Wilkinson (GBR)	6/7(12) 6/7(2) L		3/6 6/7(2) L	6/3 6/4 W	1	2
L. Jensen (USA) & M. Jensen (USA)	5/7 2/6 L	6/3 7/6(2) W		6/4 7/6(10) W	2	1
P. Aldrich (RSA) & D. Visser (RSA)	4/6 3/6 L	3/6 4/6 L	4/6 6/7(10) L		0	3

SEMI-FINAL: T.A. Woodbridge (AUS) & M. Woodforde (AUS)

GROUP B	E. Ferreira (RSA) & R. Leach (USA)	J. Grabb (USA) & R. Reneberg (USA)	B. Black (ZIM) & M. Pernfors (SWE)	J. Frana (ARG) & L. Lavalle (MEX)	WINS	LOSSES
E. Ferreira (RSA) & R. Leach (USA)		7/5 6/3 W	7/6(5) 7/5 W	6/3 6/4 W	3	0
J. Grabb (USA) & R. Reneberg (USA)	5/7 3/6 L		6/3 4/6 7/5 W	6/1 6/2 W	2	1
B. Black (ZIM) & M. Pernfors (SWE)	6/7(5) 5/7 L	3/6 6/4 5/7 L		6/3 6/4 W	1	2
J. Frana (ARG) & L. Lavalle (MEX)	3/6 4/6 L	1/6 2/6 L	3/6 4/6 L		0	3

SEMI-FINAL: E. Ferreira (RSA) & R. Leach (USA)

Final between T.A. Woodbridge (AUS) & M. Woodforde (AUS): 6/3 3/6 6/4

GROUP C	J. Eltingh (NED) & P. Haarhuis (NED)	A. Jarryd (SWE) & C. Pioline (FRA)	K. Flach (USA) & N. Fulwood (GBR)	P. Galbraith (USA) & S. Melville (USA)	WINS	LOSSES
J. Eltingh (NED) & P. Haarhuis (NED)		4/6 6/7(3) L	6/3 7/5 W	6/4 6/3 W	2	1
A. Jarryd (SWE) & C. Pioline (FRA)	6/4 7/6(3) W		6/4 7/6(7) W	6/2 7/6(3) W	3	0
K. Flach (USA) & N. Fulwood (GBR)	3/6 5/7 L	4/6 6/7(7) L		3/6 4/6 L	0	3
P. Galbraith (USA) & S. Melville (USA)	4/6 3/6 L	2/6 6/7(3) L	6/3 6/4 W		1	2

SEMI-FINAL: A. Jarryd (SWE) & C. Pioline (FRA)

GROUP D	G. Ivanisevic (CRO) & H. Leconte (FRA)	T-J. Middleton (USA) & D. Wheaton (USA)	N. Broad (GBR) & M. Petchey (GBR)	G.W. Donnelly (USA) & S. Zivojinovic (SCG)	WINS	LOSSES
G. Ivanisevic (CRO) & H. Leconte (FRA)		4/6 4/6 L	7/6(5) 6/3 W	7/5 6/3 W	2	1
T-J. Middleton (USA) & D. Wheaton (USA)	6/4 6/4 W		6/3 6/2 W	7/6(4) 6/1 W	3	0
N. Broad (GBR) & M. Petchey (GBR)	6/7(5) 3/6 L	3/6 2/6 L		6/1 6/2 W	1	2
G.W. Donnelly (USA) & S. Zivojinovic (SCG)	5/7 3/6 L	6/7(4) 1/6 L	1/6 2/6 L		0	3

SEMI-FINAL: T-J. Middleton (USA) & D. Wheaton (USA)

Semi-finals:
T.A. Woodbridge (AUS) & M. Woodforde (AUS) beat A. Jarryd (SWE) & C. Pioline (FRA) 6/3 7/6(3)
E. Ferreira (RSA) & R. Leach (USA) / T-J. Middleton (USA) & D. Wheaton (USA) 6/3 7/6(3)

FINAL: T.A. Woodbridge (AUS) & M. Woodforde (AUS) 6/7(5) 7/5 7/6(4)

This event was played on a 'round robin' basis. 16 invited pairs were divided into 4 groups and each pair in each group played one another.

The pairs winning most matches were the winners of their respective groups and played semi-final and final rounds as indicated above.

If matches should be equal in any group, the head to head result between the two pairs with the same number of wins, determined the winning pair of the group.

Heavy type denotes seeded players. The matches were the best of three sets. The tie-break operated at six games all in all three sets.

ALPHABETICAL LIST – 35 & OVER EVENTS
GENTLEMEN

Aldrich P. (*South Africa*)
Bates M.J. (*Great Britain*)
Black B. (*Zimbabwe*)
Broad N. (*Great Britain*)
Donnelly G.W. (*USA*)
Eltingh J. (*Netherlands*)
Ferreira E. (*South Africa*)
Flach K. (*USA*)

Frana J. (*Argentina*)
Fulwood N. (*Great Britain*)
Galbraith P. (*USA*)
Grabb J. (*USA*)
Haarhuis P. (*Netherlands*)
Ivanisevic G. (*Croatia*)
Jarryd A. (*Sweden*)
Jensen L. (*USA*)

Jensen M. (*USA*)
Lavalle L. (*Mexico*)
Leach R. (*USA*)
Leconte H. (*France*)
Melville S. (*USA*)
Middleton T-J. (*USA*)
Pernfors M. (*Sweden*)
Petchey M. (*Great Britain*)

Pioline C. (*France*)
Reneberg R. (*USA*)
Visser D. (*South Africa*)
Wheaton D. (*USA*)
Wilkinson C. (*Great Britain*)
Woodbridge T.A. (*Australia*)
Woodforde M. (*Australia*)
Zivojinovic S. (*Serbia and Montegro*)

LADIES

Arendt Miss N. (*USA*)
Austin Miss T. (*USA*)
Bollegraf Miss M.M. (*Netherlands*)
Durie Miss J.M. (*Great Britain*)

Jausovec Miss M. (*Slovenia*)
Kloss Miss I. (*South Africa*)
Magers Mrs G. (*USA*)
Mandlikova Miss H. (*Australia*)

McNeill Miss L. (*USA*)
Nideffer Mrs R.D. (*USA*)
Novotna Miss J. (*Czech Republic*)
Rinaldi Mrs K. (*USA*)

Smylie Mrs E.M. (*Australia*)
Sukova Miss H. (*Czech Republic*)
Tauziat Miss N. (*France*)
Turnbull Miss W.M. (*Australia*)

ALPHABETICAL LIST – 45 & OVER EVENT
GENTLEMEN

Alexander J.G. (*Australia*)
Amritraj A. (*India*)
Amritraj V. (*India*)
Bahrami M. (*Iran*)
Curren K. (*USA*)
Dent P. (*Australia*)

Dowdeswell C. (*Great Britain*)
Fitzgerald J.B. (*Australia*)
Fleming P. (*USA*)
Gottfried B.E. (*USA*)
Guenthardt H. (*Switzerland*)
Gullikson T.R. (*USA*)

Kriek J. (*USA*)
Lloyd J.M. (*Great Britain*)
Mayer G. (*USA*)
Mayer A. (*USA*)
McNamara P.B. (*Australia*)
McNamee P.F. (*Australia*)

Nastase I. (*Romania*)
Ramirez R. (*Mexico*)
Smith S.R. (*USA*)
Stockton R.L. (*USA*)
Taroczy B. (*Hungary*)
Vilas G. (*Argentina*)

EVENT VII – THE 45 AND OVER GENTLEMEN'S INVITATION DOUBLES 2006
HOLDERS: K. CURREN & J. KRIEK

The Winners became the holders, for the year only, of a Cup presented by The All England Lawn Tennis and Croquet Club. The Winners received miniature silver salvers. A Silver Medal was presented to each of the Runners-up.

GROUP A	K. Curren (USA) & J. Kriek (USA)	C. Dowdeswell (GBR) & G. Vilas (ARG)	H. Guenthardt (SUI) & B. Taroczy (HUN)	WINS	LOSSES
K. Curren (USA) & J. Kriek (USA)		6/4 6/3 W	6/3 6/1 W	2	0
C. Dowdeswell (GBR) & G. Vilas (ARG)	4/6 3/6 L		5/7 6/2 5/4 Ret'd W	1	1
H. Guenthardt (SUI) & B. Taroczy (HUN)	3/6 1/6 L	7/5 2/6 4/5 Ret'd L		0	2

GROUP B	T.R. Gullikson (USA) & R.L. Stockton (USA)	J.G. Alexander (AUS) & P. Dent (AUS)	I. Nastase (ROM) & S.R. Smith (USA)	WINS	LOSSES
T.R. Gullikson (USA) & R.L. Stockton (USA)		4/6 4/6 L	6/2 6/4 W	1	1
J.G. Alexander (AUS) & P. Dent (AUS)	6/4 6/4 W		6/3 7/6(2) W	2	0
I. Nastase (ROM) & S.R. Smith (USA)	2/6 4/6 L	3/6 6/7(2) L		0	2

GROUP C	M. Bahrami (IRI) & G. Mayer (USA)	A. Amritraj (IND) & V. Amritraj (IND)	B.E. Gottfried (USA) & R. Ramirez (MEX)	WINS	LOSSES
M. Bahrami (IRI) & G. Mayer (USA)		6/2 7/6(5) W	6/2 6/2 W	2	0
A. Amritraj (IND) & V. Amritraj (IND)	2/6 6/7(5) L		6/3 6/4 W	1	1
B.E. Gottfried (USA) & R. Ramirez (MEX)	2/6 2/6 L	3/6 4/6 L		0	2

GROUP D	P.B. McNamara (AUS) & P.F. McNamee (AUS)	J.B. Fitzgerald (AUS) & J.M. Lloyd (GBR)	P. Fleming (USA) & A. Mayer (USA)	WINS	LOSSES
P.B. McNamara (AUS) & P.F. McNamee (AUS)		6/3 6/4 W	6/3 7/6(4) W	2	0
J.B. Fitzgerald (AUS) & J.M. Lloyd (GBR)	3/6 4/6 L		3/6 7/5 L	0	2
P. Fleming (USA) & A. Mayer (USA)	3/6 6/7(4) L	6/3 7/5 W		1	1

SEMI-FINAL

K. Curren (USA) & J. Kriek (USA)

J.G. Alexander (AUS) & P. Dent (AUS)

M. Bahrami (IRI) & G. Mayer (USA)

P.B. McNamara (AUS) & P.F. McNamee (AUS)

K. Curren (USA) & J. Kriek (USA) 6/3 6/3

P.B. McNamara (AUS) & P.F. McNamee (AUS) 7/6 (5) 7/5

FINAL

K. Curren (USA) & J. Kriek (USA) 7/5 6/7(8) 7/6(9)

This event was played on a 'round robin' basis. 12 invited pairs were divided into 4 groups and each pair in each group played one another.
The pairs winning most matches were the winners of their respective groups and played semi-final and final rounds as indicated above.
If matches should be equal in any group, the head to head result between the two pairs with the same number of wins, will determine the winning pair of the group.
Heavy type denotes seeded players. The matches were the best of three sets. The tie-break operated at six games all in all three sets.

EVENT VII – THE 35 AND OVER LADIES INVITATION DOUBLES 2006
HOLDERS: MISS T. AUSTIN & MISS J. NOVOTNA

The Winners became the holders, for the year only, of a Cup presented by The All England Lawn Tennis and Croquet Club. The Winners received miniature Cups. A Silver Medal was presented to each of the Runners-up.

GROUP A	Mrs R.D. Nideffer (USA) & Miss J. Novotna (CZE)	Miss N. Arendt (USA) & Miss I. Kloss (RSA)	Miss J.M. Durie (GBR) & Mrs K. Rinaldi (USA)	Mrs G. Magers (USA) & Mrs E.M. Smylie (AUS)	WINS	LOSSES
Mrs R.D. Nideffer (USA) & Miss J. Novotna (CZE)		6/4 6/2 W	6/2 7/6(4) W	7/5 6/2 W	3	0
Miss N. Arendt (USA) & Miss I. Kloss (RSA)	4/6 2/6 L		w/o L	7/5 3/6 4/6 L	0	3
Miss J.M. Durie (GBR) & Mrs K. Rinaldi (USA)	2/6 6/7(4) L	w/o W		4/6 2/6 L	1	2
Mrs G. Magers (USA) & Mrs E.M. Smylie (AUS)	5/7 2/6 L	5/7 6/3 6/4 W	6/4 6/2 W		2	1

GROUP B	Miss T. Austin (USA) & Miss N. Tauziat (FRA)	Miss M.M. Bollegraf (NED) & Miss W.M. Turnbull (AUS)	Miss M. Jausovec (SLO) & Miss H. Sukova (CZE)	Miss H. Mandlikova (AUS) & Miss L. McNeill (USA)	WINS	LOSSES
Miss T. Austin (USA) & Miss N. Tauziat (FRA)		6/2 6/0 W	6/3 6/2 W	1/0 Ret'd W	3	0
Miss M.M. Bollegraf (NED) & Miss W.M. Turnbull (AUS)	2/6 0/6 L		7/6(3) 4/6 0/6 L	3/6 4/6 L	0	3
Miss M. Jausovec (SLO) & Miss H. Sukova (CZE)	3/6 2/6 L	6/7(3) 6/4 6/0 W		6/7(3) 7/6(5) 6/7(5) L	1	2
Miss H. Mandlikova (AUS) & Miss L. McNeill (USA)	0/1 Ret'd L	6/3 6/4 W	7/6(3) 6/7(5) 7/6(5) W		2	1

FINAL

Mrs R.D. Nideffer (USA) & Miss J. Novotna (CZE)

Miss T. Austin (USA) & Miss N. Tauziat (FRA)

Mrs R.D. Nideffer (USA) & Miss J. Novotna (CZE) 6/4 6/3

This event was played on a 'round robin' basis. 8 invited pairs were divided into 2 groups of 4 and each pair in each group played one another.
The pairs winning most matches were the winners of their respective groups and played a final round as indicated above.
If matches should be equal in any group, the head to head result between the two pairs with the same number of wins, will determine the winning pair of the group.
Heavy type denotes seeded players. The matches were the best of three sets. The tie-break operated at six games all in all three sets.

EVENT IX – THE WHEELCHAIR GENTLEMEN'S DOUBLES 2006
HOLDERS: M. JEREMIASZ & J. MISTRY

The Winners received Silver Salvers.

Third & Fourth Place Play-off

R.Ammerlaan (NED) & M.Legner (AUT) [2] 6/3 6/1

M.Brychta (CZE) & T.Kruszelnicki (POL)

R.Ammerlaan (NED) & M.Legner (AUT) [2]

First Round

1. S.Kunieda (JPN) & S.Saida (JPN) [1]

2. M.Brychta (CZE) & T.Kruszelnicki (POL)

3. M.Jeremiasz (FRA) & J.Mistry (GBR)

4. R.Ammerlaan (NED) & M.Legner (AUT) [2]

Final

S.Kunieda (JPN) & S.Saida (JPN) [1] 1/6 6/2 6/2

M.Jeremiasz (FRA) & J.Mistry (GBR) 6/1 6/3

S.Kunieda (JPN) & S.Saida (JPN) [1] 7/5 6/2

Heavy type denotes seeded players. The figure in brackets against names denotes the order in which they have been seeded.

EVENT X – THE BOYS' SINGLES CHAMPIONSHIP 2006
HOLDER: J. CHARDY

The Winner became the holder, for the year only, of a Cup presented by The All England Lawn Tennis and Croquet Club. The Winner received a miniature Cup and the Runner-up received a memento. The matches were best of three sets.

First Round
1. De Bakker, Thiemo [1] (NED)
2. Bai, Yan (CHN)
(Q) 3. Elias, Gastao (POR)
4. Veic, Antonio (CRO)
(WC) 5. Rice, David (GBR)
6. Massa, Emiliano (ARG)
(WC) 7. Beidas, Bassam (LIB)
(WC) 8. Silva, Daniel [16] (BRA)
9. Chernov, Artur [12] (RUS)
10. Botti, Kevin (FRA)
11. Hunt, Jamie (USA)
12. Lemke, James (AUS)
13. Gemouchidis, Paris (GRE)
14. Bautista-Agut, Roberto (ESP)
15. Maytin, Roberto (VEN)
16. Singh, Sanam K [8] (IND)
(WC) 17. Young, Donald [3] (USA)
(WC) 18. Atkinson, Iain (GBR)
19. Ramos-Vinolas, Albert (ESP)
20. Aidil, Faisal (INA)
21. Lopez, Daniel (ITA)
22. Podlipnik, Hans (CHI)
23. Panfil, Grzegorz (POL)
24. Roshardt, Robin [15] (SUI)
25. Sergeyev, Ivan [9] (UKR)
26. Konecny, Michal (CZE)
27. Martin, Andrei (SVK)
28. Roy, Rupesh (IND)
29. Klein, Brydon (AUS)
30. Lajola, Dennis (USA)
(Q) 31. Velasco, Jose-Roberto (BOL)
32. Luncanu, Petru [7] (ROM)
33. Belic, Luka [6] (CRO)
34. Donald, Stephen (AUS)
(WC) 35. Dyce, Graham (GBR)
36. Bowles, Clint (USA)
37. Koniusz, Blazej (POL)
(Q) 38. Xu, Junchao (CHN)
39. Vitulli, Christian (KEN)
40. Lee, Hsin Han [10] (TPE)
41. Nedunchezhiya, Jeevan [14] (IND)
(WC) 42. Corrie, Ed (GBR)
(Q) 43. Smith, John-Patrick (AUS)
44. Lucassen, Peter (NED)
45. Bester, Philip (CAN)
46. Garrapiz-Borderias, Javier (ESP)
47. Chekhov, Pavel (RUS)
48. Sidorenko, Alexandre [4] (FRA)
49. Santos, Nicolas [5] (BRA)
(Q) 50. Gawron, Marcin (POL)
51. Damico, Kellen (USA)
52. Fabbiano, Thomas (ITA)
53. Jones, Greg (AUS)
(Q) 54. Urzua, Ricardo (CHI)
(Q) 55. Sessagesimi, Dylan 'Loic' (SUI)
56. Aida, Sho [11] (JPN)
57. Jebavy, Roman [13] (CZE)
58. Sousa, Pedro (POR)
59. Mektic, Nikola (CRO)
60. Schnugg, Nathaniel (USA)
(WC) 61. Cox, Daniel (GBR)
(Q) 62. Rodriguez, Edgar (COL)
63. Poldma, Jaak (EST)
64. Klizan, Martin [2] (SVK)

Second Round
T.De Bakker [1] 6/1 6/0
A.Veic 6/4 6/3
E.Massa 7/6(5) 6/3
D.Silva [16] 7/5 6/3
A.Chernov [12] 3/6 6/4 6/4
J.Hunt 6/3 5/7 6/3
R.Bautista-Agut 6/4 6/2
S.K.Singh [8] 6/1 6/2
D.O.Young [3] 6/2 7/6(2)
A.Ramos-Vinolas 6/4 3/6 6/0
D.Lopez 6/3 6/4
R.Roshardt [15] 6/3 7/5
M.Konecny 6/3 6/3
A.Martin 6/2 7/5
B.Klein 6/3 6/1
P.Luncanu [7] 6/1 5/7 6/3
L.Belic [6] 6/2 6/1
C.Bowles 7/6(4) 6/4
J.Xu 6/3 6/0
H.H.Lee [10] 6/3 7/6(6)
E.Corrie 6/0 6/7(4) 6/1
P.Lucassen 6/4 2/6 6/2
P.Bester 6/7(9) 6/3 7/5
P.Chekhov 1/6 6/3 6/4
M.Gawron 7/5 6/4
K.Damico 6/4 6/4
G.Jones 6/1 6/1
D.Sessagesimi 6/3 6/3
P.Sousa 7/5 6/4
N.Mektic 6/1 5/7 6/1
D.Cox 6/1 4/6 6/3
J.Poldma 6/3 3/6 6/3

Third Round
T.De Bakker [1] 6/3 4/6 6/3
E.Massa 6/4 4/6 6/3
A.Chernov [12] 6/2 6/4
S.K.Singh [8] 6/4 3/6 6/4
D.O.Young [3] 6/1 6/4
R.Roshardt [15] 3/6 7/6(4) 7/5
M.Konecny 6/2 6/4
P.Luncanu [7] 6/4 6/0
L.Belic [6] 6/2 7/6(6)
H.H.Lee [10] 7/5 6/2
P.Lucassen 6/7(5) 6/4 6/4
P.Chekhov 6/4 6/7(3) 6/3
M.Gawron 6/4 3/6 6/3
G.Jones 7/6(4) 2/6 6/3
N.Mektic 7/5 6/2
J.Poldma 5/7 6/4 6/3

Quarter-Finals
T.De Bakker [1] 6/7(2) 6/3 6/4
A.Chernov [12] 6/2 6/3
R.Roshardt [15] 6/4 7/6(7)
M.Konecny 6/2 6/4
L.Belic [6] 6/2 6/4
P.Chekhov 6/4 6/4
M.Gawron 6/7(4) 6/4 10/8
N.Mektic 6/3 5/7 6/3

Semi-Finals
T.De Bakker [1] 6/2 6/2
M.Konecny 3/0 Ret'd
P.Chekhov 6/4 6/4
M.Gawron 6/3 6/4

Final
T.De Bakker [1] 7/5 6/4
M.Gawron 7/6(3) 7/6(8)

Winner
T.De Bakker [1] 6/2 7/6(4)

Heavy type denotes seeded players. The figure in brackets against names denotes the order in which they were seeded.
(WC)=Wild card. (Q)=Qualifier.

EVENT XI – THE BOYS' DOUBLES CHAMPIONSHIP 2006
HOLDER: J. LEVINE & M. SHABAZ

The Winners became the holders, for the year only, of a Cup presented by The All England Lawn Tennis and Croquet Club.
The Winners received miniature Cups and the Runners-up received mementos. The matches were best of three sets.

First Round
1. T.De Bakker (NED) & A.Sidorenko (FRA) [1]
2. K.Damico (USA) & N.Schnugg (USA)
3. T.Fabbiano (ITA) & D.Lopez (ITA)
4. B.Klein (AUS) & J-P.Smith (AUS)
5. K.Botti (FRA) & D.Sessagesimi (SUI)
(WC) 6. D.Rice (GBR) & D.Walsh (GBR)
7. G.Elias (POR) & P.Sousa (POR)
8. J.Poldma (EST) & I.Sergeyev (UKR) [8]
9. J.Nedunchezhiya (IND) & S.K.Singh (IND) [4]
10. N.Mektic (CRO) & V.Siljegovic (CRO)
11. Y.Bai (CHN) & N.Santos (BRA)
12. F.Aidil (INA) & J.Xu (CHN)
13. D.Lajola (USA) & C.Vitulli (KEN)
(WC) 14. D.Cox (GBR) & G.Dyce (GBR)
(WC) 15. F.Romboli (BRA) & D.Silva (BRA)
16. P.Bester (CAN) & R.Roshardt (SUI) [7]
17. S.Aida (JPN) & A.Chernov (RUS) [5]
18. E.Rodriguez (COL) & J-R.Velasco (BOL)
19. H.H.Lee (TPE) & R.Roy (IND)
(WC) 20. S.Dickson (GBR) & C.Llewellyn (GBR)
21. B.Beidas (LIB) & M.Gawron (POL)
22. J.Hunt (USA) & R.Maytin (VEN)
23. G.Jones (AUS) & J.Lemke (AUS)
24. L.Belic (CRO) & A.Veic (CRO) [3]
25. R.Jebavy (CZE) & H.Podlipnik (CHI) [6]
26. S.Donald (AUS) & M.Konecny (CZE)
27. D.Koniusz (POL) & G.Panfil (POL)
28. J.Garrapiz-Borderias (ESP) & A.Ramos-Vinolas (ESP)
29. P.Lucassen (NED) & P.Luncanu (ROM)
30. P.Chekhov (RUS) & E.Massa (ARG)
31. P.Gemouchidis (GRE) & R.Urzua (CHI)
32. M.Klizan (SVK) & A.Martin (SVK) [2]

Second Round
K.Damico & N.Schnugg 6/4 3/6 7/5
B.Klein & J-P.Smith 4/6 7/6(6) 6/3
D.Rice & D.Walsh 7/6(5) 6/4
G.Elias & P.Sousa 2/6 7/5 9/7
N.Mektic & V.Siljegovic 7/6(4) 6/4
F.Aidil & J.Xu 5/7 6/3 7/5
D.Lajola & C.Vitulli 6/2 6/3
F.Romboli & D.Silva 4/6 6/4 6/4
E.Rodriguez & J-R.Velasco 1/6 6/3 6/4
H.H.Lee & R.Roy 6/2 6/3
J.Hunt & R.Maytin 6/1 6/4
L.Belic & A.Veic [3] 5/7 6/4 6/4
S.Donald & M.Konecny 6/4 6/1
J.Garrapiz-Borderias & A.Ramos-Vinolas 7/5 6/4
P.Lucassen & P.Luncanu w/o
M.Klizan & A.Martin [2] 7/5 7/5

Quarter-Finals
K.Damico & N.Schnugg 3/6 6/3 6/4
G.Elias & P.Sousa 6/1 6/4
N.Mektic & V.Siljegovic 6/4 6/3
D.Lajola & C.Vitulli 7/5 1/0 Ret'd
H.H.Lee & R.Roy 6/7(2) 6/3 6/4
L.Belic & A.Veic [3] 6/2 2/6 6/2
J.Garrapiz-Borderias & A.Ramos-Vinolas 7/6(6) 6/7(4) 9/7
M.Klizan & A.Martin [2] 7/6(5) 6/2

Semi-Finals
K.Damico & N.Schnugg 6/7(3) 6/4 6/3
N.Mektic & V.Siljegovic 6/4 6/4
H.H.Lee & R.Roy 7/6(5) 6/7(4) 6/4
M.Klizan & A.Martin [2] 6/4 6/3

Final
K.Damico & N.Schnugg 6/3 3/6 6/0
M.Klizan & A.Martin [2] 6/3 6/7(4) 6/3

Winner
K.Damico & N.Schnugg 7/6(7) 6/2

Heavy type denotes seeded players. The figure in brackets against names denotes the order in which they were seeded.
(WC)=Wild card.

EVENT XII – THE GIRLS' SINGLES CHAMPIONSHIP 2006
HOLDER: MISS A. RADWANSKA

The Winner became the holder, for the year only, of a Cup presented by The All England Lawn Tennis and Croquet Club.
The Winner received a miniature Cup and the Runner-up received a memento. The matches were best of three sets.

First Round	Second Round	Third Round	Quarter-Finals	Semi-Finals	Final	Winner
1. Pavlyuchenkova, Anastasia [1] (RUS)						
2. Kucova, Kristina (SVK)	Miss K.Kucova 6/1 7/6(10)					
3. Zhang, Ling (HKG)		Miss K.Kucova 6/2 6/4				
(WC) 4. Saidkhodjayeva, Dilyara (UZB)	Miss D.Saidkhodjayeva 6/4 7/6(6)					
(WC) 5. Cavaday, Naomi (GBR)			Miss N.Cavaday 6/3 7/6(5)			
6. Brengle, Madison (USA)	Miss N.Cavaday 6/4 6/3					
7. Lykina, Ksenia (RUS)		Miss N.Cavaday 6/4 2/6 6/1				
8. Vankova, Katerina [13] (CZE)	Miss K.Lykina 3/6 7/6(1) 8/6					
9. Pereira, Teliana [12] (BRA)				Miss U.Radwanska 6/3 6/2		
10. Pulido-Velasco, Valeria (MEX)	Miss V.Pulido-Velasco 6/3 1/6 7/5					
11. Burdette, Lyndsay (USA)		Miss T.Calderwood 6/1 5/7 6/2				
(Q) 12. Calderwood, Tyra (AUS)	Miss T.Calderwood 6/3 6/4					
13. Gaverova, Maya (RUS)			Miss U.Radwanska 7/5 6/3			
14. Radwanska, Urszula (POL)	Miss U.Radwanska 6/0 6/1					
(WC) 15. Clarke, Yasmin (GBR)		Miss U.Radwanska 6/4 6/1				
16. Cirstea, Sorana-Mihaela [5] (ROM)	Miss S-M.Cirstea [5] 6/3 2/6 6/3					
17. Wozniacki, Caroline [4] (DEN)	Miss C.Wozniacki [4] 5/7 6/1 6/2					
(WC) 18. Stoop, Georgie (GBR)		Miss C.Wozniacki [4] 6/2 6/3				
19. Jones, Sacha (NZL)	Miss S.Jones 6/3 7/6(1)					
20. Duarte, Ana-Clara (BRA)			Miss C.Wozniacki [4] 4/6 6/2 6/3			
21. Boonstra, Marrit (NED)	Miss M.Boonstra 7/5 6/2					
(Q) 22. Litvak, Lena (USA)		Miss E.Rodina [15] 6/2 6/2				
(Q) 23. Tuohimaa, Katarina (FIN)	Miss E.Rodina [15] 6/3 6/2					
24. Rodina, Evgeniya [15] (RUS)				Miss C.Wozniacki [4] 7/6(6) 6/2		
25. Milevskaya, Ksenia [11] (BLR)		Miss N.Hofmanova 6/4 3/1 Ret'd				
26. Hofmanova, Nikola (AUT)	Miss N.Hofmanova 2/6 6/2 6/4					
27. Tatishvili, Anna (GEO)			Miss A.Morita [7] 6/0 5/7 6/1			
28. Zoric, Natasa (SCG)	Miss A.Tatishvili 5/7 7/6(5) 6/4					
29. Dy, Denise (PHI)		Miss A.Morita [7] 6/2 6/3				
(WC) 30. Brook, Victoria (GBR)	Miss D.Dy 6/1 7/5					
31. Rodionova, Arina (RUS)					Miss C.Wozniacki [4] 3/6 6/7(4) 6/3	
32. Morita, Ayumi [7] (JPN)	Miss A.Morita [7] 6/2 6/0					
33. Rybarikova, Magdalena [6] (SVK)	Miss M.Rybarikova [6] 6/3 6/4					
34. Rakhim, Amina (KAZ)		Miss M.Rybarikova [6] 6/1 6/3				
35. Wickmayer, Yanina (BEL)	Miss K.Pervak 3/6 6/1 6/2					
(WC) 36. Pervak, Ksenia (RUS)			Miss M.Rybarikova [6] 6/3 6/2			
37. Gullickson, Chelsey (USA)	Miss C.Gullickson 6/3 7/6(1)					
38. Moore, Jessica (AUS)		Miss K.Antoniychuk [9] 5/7 6/3 6/1				
(Q) 39. Berkova, Andrea (CZE)	Miss K.Antoniychuk [9] 6/2 6/2					
40. Antoniychuk, Kristina [9] (UKR)				Miss M.Rybarikova [6] 7/5 4/6 6/3		
41. Erakovic, Marina [14] (NZL)	Miss J.Bone 7/5 2/0 Ret'd					
(Q) 42. Bone, Julia (GBR)		Miss J.Bone 6/4 6/2				
43. Chan, Wing Yau Venise (HKG)	Miss C.Dentoni 6/2 6/4					
44. Dentoni, Corinna (ITA)			Miss A.Kleybanova [3] 6/2 6/1			
45. Vaisemburg, Roxane (BRA)	Miss M.Klaffner 6/3 6/3					
(Q) 46. Klaffner, Melanie (AUT)		Miss A.Kleybanova [3] 6/4 7/5				
47. Palkina, Ksenia (KGZ)					Miss T.Paszek [10] 6/4 6/4	
48. Kleybanova, Alisa [3] (RUS)	Miss A.Kleybanova [3] 6/1 6/3					
49. Cohen, Julia [8] (USA)	Miss J.Cohen [8] 4/6 6/3 8/6					
(WC) 50. Ripoll, Dominice (GER)		Miss K.Kramperova 2/6 6/2 6/1				
(Q) 51. Kramperova, Katerina (CZE)	Miss K.Kramperova 6/2 6/3					
52. Tigu, Anouk (NED)			Miss T.Paszek [10] 6/4 6/2			
53. Mosolova, Maria (RUS)	Miss M.Mosolova 6/3 6/2					
54. Davin, Suzelle (NAM)		Miss T.Paszek [10] 6/0 6/1				
(WC) 55. Curtis, Jade (GBR)	Miss T.Paszek [10] 6/2 6/3					
56. Paszek, Tamira [10] (AUT)				Miss T.Paszek [10] 6/4 6/4		
57. Dulgheru, Alexandra [16] (ROM)	Miss A.Dulgheru [16] 6/1 6/0					
58. Pochakova, Michaela (SVK)		Miss A.Dulgheru [16] 7/5 6/0				
59. Panova, Alexandra (RUS)	Miss A.Panova 6/4 7/6(5)					
60. Couts, Kimberley (USA)			Miss A.Dulgheru [16] 6/2 6/4			
(WC) 61. Armstrong, Deborah (GBR)	Miss A.Pivovarova 7/6(3) 6/2					
(Q) 62. Pivovarova, Anastasia (RUS)		Miss Y-J.Chan [2] 6/3 6/2				
63. Bhambri, Sanaa (IND)						Miss C.Wozniacki [4] 3/6 6/1 6/3
64. Chan, Yung-Jan [2] (TPE)	Miss Y-J.Chan [2] 6/1 6/2					

Heavy type denotes seeded players. The figure in brackets against names denotes the order in which they were seeded.
(WC)=Wild card. (Q)=Qualifier.

EVENT XIII – THE GIRLS' DOUBLES CHAMPIONSHIP 2006
HOLDERS: MISS V. AZARENKA & MISS A. SZAVAY

The Winners became the holders, for the year only, of a Cup presented by The All England Lawn Tennis and Croquet Club.
The Winners received miniature Cups and the Runners-up received mementoes. The matches were best of three sets.

First Round	Second Round	Quarter-Finals	Semi-Finals	Final	Winner
1. Miss K.Antoniychuk (UKR) & Miss A.Dulgheru (ROM) [1]					
(WC) 2. Miss H.James (GBR) & Miss J.Rae (GBR)	Miss K.Antoniychuk & Miss A.Dulgheru [1] 6/3 6/2				
3. Miss S.Bhambri (IND) & Miss W.Y.V.Chan (HKG)		Miss K.Antoniychuk & Miss A.Dulgheru [1] 6/3 6/4			
(WC) 4. Miss A.Cunningham (GBR) & Miss J.Jackson (GBR)	Miss S.Bhambri & Miss W.Y.V.Chan 6/2 6/0				
5. Miss M.Mosolova (RUS) & Miss A.Pivovarova (RUS)			Miss K.Antoniychuk & Miss A.Dulgheru [1] 7/6(6) 6/2		
6. Miss E.Rodina (RUS) & Miss K.Vankova (CZE)	Miss M.Mosolova & Miss A.Pivovarova wo.				
7. Miss L.Burdette (USA) & Miss R.Vaisemburg (BRA)		Miss L.Burdette & Miss R.Vaisemburg 6/3 6/3			
8. Miss K.Kucova (SVK) & Miss M.Pochakova (SVK) [6]	Miss L.Burdette & Miss R.Vaisemburg 6/2				
9. Miss S-M.Cirstea (ROM) & Miss A.Panova (RUS) [4]				Miss K.Antoniychuk & Miss A.Dulgheru [1] 6/2 6/4	
10. Miss N.Cavaday (GBR) & Miss N.Zoric (SCG)	Miss S-M.Cirstea & Miss A.Panova [4] 4/6 6/1 7/5				
(WC) 11. Miss J.Curtis (GBR) & Miss G.Stoop (GBR)		Miss S-M.Cirstea & Miss A.Panova [4] 6/4 6/3			
12. Miss K.Lykina (RUS) & Miss A.Tigu (NED)	Miss J.Curtis & Miss G.Stoop 6/3 6/2				
13. Miss N.Hofmanova (AUT) & Miss M.Klaffner (AUT)			Miss S-M.Cirstea & Miss A.Panova [4] 6/4 6/3		
14. Miss T.Calderwood (AUS) & Miss K.Kramperova (CZE)	Miss T.Calderwood & Miss K.Kramperova 6/4 6/4				
15. Miss D.Dy (PHI) & Miss L.Zhang (HKG)		Miss K.Milevskaya & Miss A.Rakhim [5] 6/3 6/4			
16. Miss K.Milevskaya (BLR) & Miss A.Rakhim (KAZ) [5]	Miss K.Milevskaya & Miss A.Rakhim [5] 3/6 6/2 7/5				
17. Miss S.Jones (NZL) & Miss Y.Wickmayer (BEL) [7]				Miss S-M.Cirstea & Miss A.Panova [4] 6/4 6/4	
18. Miss U.Radwanska (POL) & Miss A.Rodionova (RUS)	Miss U.Radwanska & Miss A.Rodionova 6/3 6/0				
19. Miss K.Palkina (KGZ) & Miss D.Ripoll (GER)		Miss U.Radwanska & Miss A.Rodionova 7/6(5) 6/2			
20. Miss S.Davin (NAM) & Miss K.McVitty (USA)	Miss K.Palkina & Miss D.Ripoll 6/2 6/2				
21. Miss A-C.Duarte (BRA) & Miss L.Peterzan (GBR)			Miss U.Radwanska & Miss A.Rodionova 3/6 7/5 8/6		
(WC) 22. Miss J.Bone (GBR) & Miss L.Peterzan (GBR)	Miss A-C.Duarte & Miss T.Pereira 4/6 6/1				
23. Miss L.Litvak (USA) & Miss K.Tuohimaa (FIN)		Miss M.Boonstra & Miss C.Wozniacki [3] 4/6 6/1 7/5			
24. Miss M.Boonstra (NED) & Miss C.Wozniacki (DEN) [3]	Miss M.Boonstra & Miss C.Wozniacki [3] 6/0 6/3				
25. Miss J.Cohen (USA) & Miss K.Couts (USA) [8]			Miss A.Kleybanova & Miss A.Pavlyuchenkova [2] 6/1 6/3		
(A) 26. Miss D.Armstrong (GBR) & Miss V.Brook (GBR)	Miss J.Cohen & Miss K.Couts [8] 6/1 6/4				
27. Miss T.Paszek (AUT) & Miss A.Tatishvili (GEO)		Miss J.Cohen & Miss K.Couts [8] 6/2 6/0			
28. Miss A.Berkova (CZE) & Miss K.Pervak (RUS)	Miss A.Berkova & Miss K.Pervak wo.				
29. Miss J.Moore (AUS) & Miss V.Pulido-Velasco (MEX)			Miss A.Kleybanova & Miss A.Pavlyuchenkova [2] 6/4 6/3		
30. Miss Y.Clarke (GBR) & Miss C.Dentoni (ITA)	Miss J.Moore & Miss V.Pulido-Velasco 6/0 6/3				
31. Miss M.Gaverova (RUS) & Miss D.Saidkhodjayeva (UZB)		Miss A.Kleybanova & Miss A.Pavlyuchenkova [2] 6/4 6/2			
32. Miss A.Kleybanova (RUS) & Miss A.Pavlyuchenkova (RUS) [2]	Miss A.Kleybanova & Miss A.Pavlyuchenkova [2] 6/4 6/2				

Final: Miss K.Antoniychuk & Miss A.Dulgheru [1] 6/2 6/4; Miss A.Kleybanova & Miss A.Pavlyuchenkova [2] 7/6(4) 7/6(1)

Winner: Miss A.Kleybanova & Miss A.Pavlyuchenkova [2] 6/1 6/2

Heavy type denotes seeded players. The figure in brackets against names denotes the order in which they were seeded.
(A)=Alternates. (WC)=Wild card.

THE CHAMPIONSHIP ROLL

GENTLEMEN'S SINGLES — CHAMPIONS & RUNNERS UP

1877 S. W. Gore *W. C. Marshall*	1901 A. W. Gore *R. F. Doherty*	* 1929 H. Cochet *J. Borotra*	* 1959 A. Olmedo *R. Laver*	1983 J. P. McEnroe *C. J. Lewis*
1878 P. F. Hadow *S. W. Gore*	1902 H. L. Doherty *A. W. Gore*	1930 W. T. Tilden *W. Allison*	* 1960 N. A. Fraser *R. Laver*	1984 J. P. McEnroe *J. S. Connors*
* 1879 J. T. Hartley *V. St. L. Goold*	1903 H. L. Doherty *F. L. Riseley*	* 1931 S. B. Wood *F. X. Shields*	1961 R. Laver *C. R. McKinley*	1985 B. Becker *K. Curren*
1880 J. T. Hartley *H. F. Lawford*	1904 H. L. Doherty *F. L. Riseley*	1932 H. E. Vines *H. W. Austin*	1962 R. Laver *M. F. Mulligan*	1986 B.Becker *I. Lendl*
1881 W. Renshaw *J. T. Hartley*	1905 H. L. Doherty *N. E. Brookes*	1933 J. H. Crawford *H. E. Vines*	* 1963 C. R. McKinley *F. S. Stolle*	1987 P. Cash *I. Lendl*
1882 W. Renshaw *E. Renshaw*	1906 H. L. Doherty *F. L. Riseley*	1934 F. J. Perry *J. H. Crawford*	1964 R. Emerson *F. S. Stolle*	1988 S. Edberg *B. Becker*
1883 W. Renshaw *E. Renshaw*	* 1907 N. E. Brookes *A. W. Gore*	1935 F. J. Perry *G. von Cramm*	1965 R. Emerson *F. S. Stolle*	1989 B. Becker *S. Edberg*
1884 W. Renshaw *H. F. Lawford*	* 1908 A. W. Gore *H. Roper Barrett*	1936 F. J. Perry *G. von Cramm*	1966 M. Santana *R. D. Ralston*	1990 S. Edberg *B. Becker*
1885 W. Renshaw *H. F. Lawford*	1909 A. W. Gore *M. J. G. Ritchie*	* 1937 J. D. Budge *G. von Cramm*	1967 J. D. Newcombe *W. P. Bungert*	1991 M. Stich *B. Becker*
1886 W. Renshaw *H. F. Lawford*	1910 A. F. Wilding *A. W. Gore*	1938 J. D. Budge *H. W. Austin*	1968 R. Laver *A. D. Roche*	1992 A. Agassi *G. Ivanisevic*
* 1887 H. F. Lawford *E. Renshaw*	1911 A. F. Wilding *H. Roper Barrett*	* 1939 R. L. Riggs *E. T. Cooke*	1969 R. Laver *J. D. Newcombe*	1993 P. Sampras *J. Courier*
1888 E. Renshaw *H. F. Lawford*	1912 A. F. Wilding *A. W. Gore*	* 1946 Y. Petra *G. E. Brown*	1970 J. D. Newcombe *K. R. Rosewall*	1994 P. Sampras *G. Ivanisevic*
1889 W. Renshaw *E. Renshaw*	1913 A. F. Wilding *M. E. McLoughlin*	1947 J. Kramer *T. Brown*	1971 J. D. Newcombe *S. R. Smith*	1995 P. Sampras *B. Becker*
1890 W. J. Hamilton *W. Renshaw*	1914 N. E. Brookes *A. F. Wilding*	* 1948 R. Falkenburg *J. E. Bromwich*	* 1972 S. R. Smith *I. Nastase*	1996 R. Krajicek *M. Washington*
* 1891 W. Baddeley *J. Pim*	1919 G. L. Patterson *N. E. Brookes*	1949 F. R. Schroeder *J. Drobny*	* 1973 J. Kodes *A. Metreveli*	1997 P. Sampras *C. Pioline*
1892 W. Baddeley *J. Pim*	1920 W. T. Tilden *G. L. Patterson*	* 1950 B. Patty *F. A. Sedgman*	1974 J. S. Connors *K. R. Rosewall*	1998 P. Sampras *G. Ivanisevic*
1893 J. Pim *W. Baddeley*	1921 W. T. Tilden *B. I. C. Norton*	1951 R. Savitt *K. McGregor*	1975 A. R. Ashe *J. S. Connors*	1999 P. Sampras *A. Agassi*
1894 J. Pim *W. Baddeley*	*† 1922 G. L. Patterson *R. Lycett*	1952 F. A. Sedgman *J. Drobny*	1976 B. Borg *I. Nastase*	2000 P. Sampras *P. Rafter*
* 1895 W. Baddeley *W. V. Eaves*	* 1923 W. M. Johnston *F. T. Hunter*	* 1953 V. Seixas *K. Nielsen*	1977 B. Borg *J. S. Connors*	2001 G. Ivanisevic *P. Rafter*
1896 H. S. Mahony *W. Baddeley*	* 1924 J. Borotra *R. Lacoste*	1954 J. Drobny *K. R. Rosewall*	1978 B. Borg *J. S.Connors*	2002 L. Hewitt *D. Nalbandian*
1897 R. F. Doherty *H. S. Mahony*	1925 R. Lacoste *J. Borotra*	1955 T. Trabert *K. Nielsen*	1979 B. Borg *R. Tanner*	2003 R. Federer *M. Philippoussis*
1898 R. F. Doherty *H. L . Doherty*	* 1926 J. Borotra *H. Kinsey*	* 1956 L. A. Hoad *K. R. Rosewall*	1980 B. Borg *J. P. McEnroe*	2004 R. Federer *A. Roddick*
1899 R. F. Doherty *A. W. Gore*	1927 H. Cochet *J. Borotra*	1957 L. A. Hoad *A. J. Cooper*	1981 J. P. McEnroe *B. Borg*	2005 R. Federer *A. Roddick*
1900 R. F. Doherty *S. H. Smith*	1928 R. Lacoste *H. Cochet*	* 1958 A. J. Cooper *N. A. Fraser*	1982 J. S. Connors *J. P. McEnroe*	2006 R. Federer *R. Nadal*

For the years 1913, 1914 and 1919-1923 inclusive the above records include the "World's Championships on Grass" granted to The Lawn Tennis Association by The International Lawn Tennis Federation.
This title was then abolished and commencing in 1924 they became The OYcial Lawn Tennis Championships recognised by The International Lawn Tennis Federation.
Prior to 1922 the holders in the Singles Events and Gentlemen's Doubles did not compete in the Championships but met the winners of these events in the Challenge Rounds.
*† Challenge Round abolished: holders subsequently played through. * The holder did not defend the title.*

156

THE CHAMPIONSHIP ROLL
LADIES' SINGLES—CHAMPIONS & RUNNERS UP

1884 Miss M. Watson
Miss L. Watson

1885 Miss M. Watson
Miss B. Bingley

1886 Miss B. Bingley
Miss M. Watson

1887 Miss L. Dod
Miss B. Bingley

1888 Miss L. Dod
Mrs. G. W. Hillyard

* 1889 Mrs. G. W. Hillyard
Miss L. Rice

* 1890 Miss L. Rice
Miss M. Jacks

* 1891 Miss L. Dod
Mrs. G. W. Hillyard

1892 Miss L. Dod
Mrs. G. W. Hillyard

1893 Miss L. Dod
Mrs. G. W. Hillyard

* 1894 Mrs. G. W. Hillyard
Miss E. L. Austin

* 1895 Miss C. Cooper
Miss H. Jackson

1896 Miss C. Cooper
Mrs. W. H.Pickering

1897 Mrs. G. W. Hillyard
Miss C. Cooper

* 1898 Miss C. Cooper
Miss L Martin

1899 Mrs. G. W. Hillyard
Miss C. Cooper

1900 Mrs. G. W. Hillyard
Miss C. Cooper

1901 Mrs. A. Sterry
Mrs. G. W. Hillyard

1902 Miss M. E. Robb
Mrs. A. Sterry

* 1903 Miss D. K. Douglass
Miss E. W. Thomson

1904 Miss D. K. Douglass
Mrs. A. Sterry

1905 Miss M. Sutton
Miss D. K. Douglass

1906 Miss D. K. Douglass
Miss M. Sutton

1907 Miss M. Sutton
Mrs. Lambert Chambers

* 1908 Mrs. A. Sterry
Miss A. M. Morton

* 1909 Miss D. P. Boothby
Miss A. M. Morton

1910 Mrs. Lambert Chambers
Miss D. P. Boothby

1911 Mrs. Lambert Chambers
Miss D. P. Boothby

* 1912 Mrs. D. R. Larcombe
Mrs. A. Sterry

* 1913 Mrs. Lambert Chambers
Mrs. R. J. McNair

1914 Mrs. Lambert Chambers
Mrs. D. R. Larcombe

1919 Mlle. S. Lenglen
Mrs. Lambert Chambers

1920 Mlle. S. Lenglen
Mrs. Lambert Chambers

1921 Mlle. S. Lenglen
Miss E. Ryan

† 1922 Mlle. S. Lenglen
Mrs. F. Mallory

1923 Mlle. S. Lenglen
Miss K. McKane

1924 Miss K. McKane
Miss H. Wills

1925 Mlle. S. Lenglen
Miss J. Fry

1926 Mrs. L. A. Godfree
Sta. L. de Alvarez

1927 Miss H. Wills
Sta. L. de Alvarez

1928 Miss H. Wills
Sta. L. de Alvarez

1929 Miss H. Wills
Miss H. H. Jacobs

1930 Mrs. F. S. Moody
Miss E. Ryan

* 1931 Fraulein C. Aussem
Fraulein H. Krahwinkel

* 1932 Mrs. F. S. Moody
Miss H. H. Jacobs

1933 Mrs. F. S. Moody
Miss D. E. Round

* 1934 Miss D. E. Round
Miss H. H. Jacobs

1935 Mrs. F. S. Moody
Miss H. H. Jacobs

* 1936 Miss H. H. Jacobs
Frau. S. Sperling

1937 Miss D. E. Round
Miss J. Jedrzejowska

* 1938 Mrs. F. S. Moody
Miss H. H. Jacobs

* 1939 Miss A. Marble
Miss K. E. Stammers

* 1946 Miss P. Betz
Miss L. Brough

* 1947 Miss M. Osborne
Miss D. Hart

1948 Miss L. Brough
Miss D. Hart

1949 Miss L. Brough
Mrs. W. du Pont

1950 Miss L. Brough
Mrs. W. du Pont

1951 Miss D. Hart
Miss S. Fry

1952 Miss M. Connolly
Miss L. Brough

1953 Miss M. Connolly
Miss D. Hart

1954 Miss M. Connolly
Miss L. Brough

* 1955 Miss L. Brough
Mrs. J. G. Fleitz

1956 Miss S. Fry
Miss A. Buxton

* 1957 Miss A. Gibson
Miss D. R. Hard

1958 Miss A. Gibson
Miss A. Mortimer

* 1959 Miss M. E. Bueno
Miss D. R. Hard

1960 Miss M. E. Bueno
Miss S. Reynolds

* 1961 Miss A. Mortimer
Miss C. C. Truman

1962 Mrs. J. R. Susman
Mrs. V. Sukova

* 1963 Miss M. Smith
Miss B. J. Moffitt

1964 Miss M. E. Bueno
Miss M. Smith

1965 Miss M. Smith
Miss M. E. Bueno

1966 Mrs. L. W. King
Miss M. E. Bueno

1967 Mrs. L. W. King
Mrs. P. F. Jones

1968 Mrs. L. W. King
Miss J. A. M. Tegart

1969 Mrs. P. F. Jones
Mrs. L. W. King

* 1970 Mrs. B. M. Court
Mrs. L. W. King

1971 Miss E. F. Goolagong
Mrs. B. M. Court

1972 Mrs. L. W. King
Miss E. F. Goolagong

1973 Mrs. L. W. King
Miss C. M. Evert

1974 Miss C. M. Evert
Mrs. O. Morozova

1975 Mrs. L. W. King
Mrs. R. Cawley

* 1976 Miss C. M. Evert
Mrs. R. Cawley

1977 Miss S. V. Wade
Miss B. F. Stove

1978 Miss M. Navratilova
Miss C. M. Evert

1979 Miss M. Navratilova
Mrs. J. M. Lloyd

1980 Mrs. R. Cawley
Mrs. J. M. Lloyd

* 1981 Mrs. J. M. Lloyd
Miss H. Mandlikova

1982 Miss M. Navratilova
Mrs. J. M. Lloyd

1983 Miss M. Navratilova
Miss A. Jaeger

1984 Miss M. Navratilova
Mrs. J. M. Lloyd

1985 Miss M. Navratilova
Mrs. J. M. Lloyd

1986 Miss M. Navratilova
Miss H. Mandlikova

1987 Miss M. Navratilova
Miss S. Graf

1988 Miss S. Graf
Miss M. Navratilova

1989 Miss S. Graf
Miss M. Navratilova

1990 Miss M. Navratilova
Miss Z. Garrison

1991 Miss S. Graf
Miss G. Sabatini

1992 Miss S. Graf
Miss M. Seles

1993 Miss S. Graf
Miss J. Novotna

1994 Miss C. Martinez
Miss M. Navratilova

1995 Miss S. Graf
Miss A. Sanchez Vicario

1996 Miss S. Graf
Miss A. Sanchez Vicario

* 1997 Miss M. Hingis
Miss J. Novotna

1998 Miss J. Novotna
Miss N. Tauziat

1999 Miss L.A. Davenport
Miss S. Graf

2000 Miss V. Williams
Miss L.A. Davenport

2001 Miss V. Williams
Miss J. Henin

2002 Miss S. Williams
Miss V. Williams

2003 Miss S. Williams
Miss V. Williams

2004 Miss M. Sharapova
Miss S. Williams

2005 Miss V. Williams
Miss L. Davenport

2006 Miss A. Mauresmo
Mrs J. Henin-Hardenne

MAIDEN NAMES OF LADY CHAMPIONS *(In the tables the following have been recorded in both married and single identities)*

Mrs. R. Cawley ....Miss E. F. Goolagong	Mrs J. Henin-Hardenne................Miss J. Henin	Mrs. O. Morozova......................Miss O. Morozova
Mrs. Lambert Chambers ....Miss D. K. Douglass	Mrs. G. W. Hillyard ....Miss B. Bingley	Mrs. L. E. G. Price ....Miss S. Reynolds
Mrs. B. M. Court ....Miss M. Smith	Mrs. P. F. Jones.......................Miss A. S. Haydon	Mrs. G. E. Reid ....Miss K. Melville
Mrs. B. C. Covell ....Miss P. L. Howkins	Mrs. L. W. King ....Miss B. J. Moffitt	Mrs. P. D. Smylie ....Miss E. M. Sayers
Mrs. D. E. Dalton ....Miss J. A. M. Tegart	Mrs. M. R. King........................Miss P. E. Mudford	Frau. S. Sperling ....Fraulein H. Krahwinkel
Mrs. W. du Pont ....Miss M. Osborne	Mrs. D. R. Larcombe ....Miss E. W. Thomson	Mrs. A. Sterry ....Miss C. Cooper
Mrs. L. A. Godfree...................Miss K. McKane	Mrs. J. M. Lloyd ....Miss C. M. Evert	Mrs. J. R. Susman ....Miss K. Hantze
Mrs. H. F. Gourlay Cawley ....Miss H. F. Gourlay	Mrs. F. S. Moody.....................Miss H. Wills	

THE CHAMPIONSHIP ROLL

GENTLEMEN'S DOUBLES—CHAMPIONS & RUNNERS UP

1879 L. R. Erskine & H. F Lawford
F Durant & G. E. Tabor

1880 W. Renshaw & E. Renshaw
O. E. Woodhouse & C. J. Cole

1881 W. Renshaw & E. Renshaw
W. J. Down & H. Vaughan

1882 J. T. Hartley & R. T. Richardson
J. G. Horn & C. B. Russell

1883 C. W. Grinstead & C. E. Welldon
C. B. Russell & R. T. Milford

1884 W. Renshaw & E. Renshaw
E. W. Lewis & E. L Williams

1885 W. Renshaw & E. Renshaw
C. E. Farrer & A. J. Stanley

1886 W. Renshaw & E. Renshaw
C. E. Farrer & A. J. Stanley

1887 P. Bowes-Lyon & H. W. W. Wilberforce
J. H. Crispe & E. Barratt Smith

1888 W. Renshaw & E. Renshaw
P Bowes-Lyon & H. W. W. Wilberforce

1889 W. Renshaw & E. Renshaw
E. W. Lewis & G. W. Hillyard

1890 J. Pim & F. O. Stoker
E. W. Lewis & G. W. Hillyard

1891 W. Baddeley & H. Baddeley
J. Pim & F. O. Stoker

1892 H. S. Barlow & E. W. Lewis
W. Baddeley & H. Baddeley

1893 J. Pim & F. O. Stoker
E. W. Lewis & H. S. Barlow

1894 W. Baddeley & H. Baddeley
H. S. Barlow & C. H. Martin

1895 W. Baddeley & H. Baddeley
E. W. Lewis & W. V. Eaves

1896 W. Baddeley & H. Baddeley
R. F. Doherty & H. A. Nisbet

1897 R. F. Doherty & H. L. Doherty
W. Baddeley & H. Baddeley

1898 R. F. Doherty & H. L . Doherty
H. A. Nisbet & C. Hobart

1899 R. F. Doherty & H. L. Doherty
H. A. Nisbet & C. Hobart

1900 R. F. Doherty & H. L. Doherty
H. Roper Barrett & H. A. Nisbet

1901 R. F. Doherty & H. L. Doherty
Dwight Davis & Holcombe Ward

1902 S. H. Smith & F. L. Riseley
R. F. Doherty & H. L. Doherty

1903 R. F. Doherty & H. L. Doherty
S. H. Smith & F. L. Riseley

1904 R. F. Doherty & H. L. Doherty
S. H. Smith & F. L. Riseley

1905 R. F. Doherty & H. L. Doherty
S. H. Smith & F. L. Riseley

1906 S. H. Smith & F. L. Riseley
R. F. Doherty & H. L. Doherty

1907 N. E. Brookes & A. F. Wilding
B. C. Wright & K. H. Behr

1908 A. F. Wilding & M. J. G. Ritchie
A. W. Gore & H. Roper Barrett

1909 A. W. Gore & H. Roper Barrett
S. N. Doust & H. A. Parker

1910 A. F. Wilding & M. J. G. Ritchie
A. W. Gore & H. Roper Barrett

1911 M. Decugis & A. H. Gobert
M. J. G. Ritchie & A. F. Wilding

1912 H. Roper Barrett & C. P. Dixon
M. Decugis & A. H. Gobert

1913 H. Roper Barrett & C. P. Dixon
F. W. Rahe & H. Kleinschroth

1914 N. E. Brookes & A. F. Wilding
H. Roper Barrett & C. P. Dixon

1919 R. V. Thomas & P. O'Hara-Wood
R. Lycett & R. W. Heath

1920 R. N. Williams & C. S. Garland
A. R. F. Kingscote & J. C. Parke

1921 R. Lycett & M. Woosnam
F. G. Lowe & A. H. Lowe

1922 R. Lycett & J. O. Anderson
G. L. Patterson & P. O'Hara-Wood

1923 R. Lycett & L. A. Godfree
Count de Gomar & E. Flaquer

1924 F. T. Hunter & V. Richards
R. N. Williams & W. M. Washburn

1925 J. Borotra & R. Lacoste
J. Hennessey & R. Casey

1926 H. Cochet & J. Brugnon
V. Richards & H. Kinsey

1927 F. T. Hunter & W. T. Tilden
J. Brugnon & H. Cochet

1928 H. Cochet & J. Brugnon
G. L. Patterson & J. B. Hawkes

1929 W. Allison & J. Van Ryn
J. C. Gregory & I. G. Collins

1930 W. Allison & J. Van Ryn
J. H. Doeg & G. M. Lott

1931 G. M Lott & J. Van Ryn
H. Cochet & J. Brugnon

1932 J. Borotra & J. Brugnon
G. P. Hughes & F. J. Perry

1933 J. Borotra & J. Brugnon
R. Nunoi & J. Satoh

1934 G. M. Lott & L. R. Stoefen
J. Borotra & J. Brugnon

1935 J. H. Crawford & A. K. Quist
W. Allison & J. Van Ryn

1936 G. P. Hughes & C. R. D. Tuckey
C. E. Hare & F. H. D. Wilde

1937 J. D. Budge & G. Mako
G. P. Hughes & C. R. D. Tuckey

1938 J. D. Budge & G. Mako
H. Henkel & G. von Metaxa

1939 R. L. Riggs & E. T. Cooke
C. E. Hare & F. H. D. Wilde

1946 T. Brown & J. Kramer
G. E. Brown & D. Pails

1947 R. Falkenburg & J. Kramer
A. J. Mottram & O. W. Sidwell

1948 J. E. Bromwich & F. A. Sedgman
T. Brown & G. Mulloy

1949 R. Gonzales & F. Parker
G. Mulloy & F. R. Schroeder

1950 J. E. Bromwich & A. K. Quist
G. E. Brown & O. W Sidwell

1951 K. McGregor & F. A. Sedgman
J. Drobny & E. W. Sturgess

1952 K. McGregor & F. A. Sedgman
V. Seixas & E. W. Sturgess

1953 L. A. Hoad & K. R. Rosewall
R. N. Hartwig & M. G. Rose

1954 R. N. Hartwig & M. G. Rose
V. Seixas & T. Trabert

1955 R. N. Hartwig & L. A. Hoad
N. A. Fraser & K. R. Rosewall

1956 L. A. Hoad & K. R. Rosewall
N. Pietrangeli & O. Sirola

1957 G. Mulloy & B. Patty
N. A. Fraser & L. A. Hoad

1958 S. Davidson & U. Schmidt
A. J. Cooper & N. A. Fraser

1959 R. Emerson & N. A. Fraser
R. Laver & R. Mark

1960 R. H. Osuna & R. D. Ralston
M. G. Davies & R. K. Wilson

1961 R. Emerson & N. A. Fraser
R. A. J. Hewitt & F. S. Stolle

1962 R. A. J. Hewitt & F. S. Stolle
B. Jovanovic & N. Pilic

1963 R. H. Osuna & A. Palafox
J. C. Barclay & P. Darmon

1964 R. A. J. Hewitt & F. S. Stolle
R. Emerson & K. N. Fletcher

1965 J. D. Newcombe & A. D. Roche
K. N. Fletcher & R. A. J. Hewitt

1966 K. N. Fletcher & J. D. Newcombe
W. W. Bowrey & O. K. Davidson

1967 R. A. J. Hewitt & F. D. McMillan
R. Emerson & K. N. Fletcher

1968 J. D. Newcombe & A. D. Roche
K. R. Rosewall & F. S. Stolle

1969 J. D. Newcombe & A. D. Roche
T. S. Okker & M. C. Reissen

1970 J. D. Newcombe & A. D. Roche
K. R. Rosewall & F. S. Stolle

1971 R. S. Emerson & R. G. Laver
A. R. Ashe & R. D. Ralston

1972 R. A. J. Hewitt & F. D. McMillan
S. R. Smith & E. J. van Dillen

1973 J. S. Connors & I. Nastase
J. R. Cooper & N. A. Fraser

1974 J. D. Newcombe & A. D. Roche
R. C. Lutz & S. R. Smith

1975 V. Gerulaitis & A. Mayer
C. Dowdeswell & A. J. Stone

1976 B. E. Gottfried & R. Ramirez
R. L. Case & G. Masters

1977 R. L. Case & G. Masters
J. G. Alexander & P. C. Dent

1978 R. A. J. Hewitt & F. D. McMillan
P. Fleming & J. P. McEnroe

1979 P. Fleming & J. P . McEnroe
B. E. Gottfried & R. Ramirez

1980 P. McNamara & P. McNamee
R. C. Lutz & S. R. Smith

1981 P. Fleming & J. P. McEnroe
R. C. Lutz & S. R. Smith

1982 P. McNamara & P. McNamee
P. Fleming & J. P. McEnroe

1983 P. Fleming & J. P. McEnroe
T. E. Gullikson & T. R. Gullikson

1984 P. Fleming & J. P. McEnroe
P. Cash & P. McNamee

1985 H. P. Guenthardt & B. Taroczy
P. Cash & J. B. Fitzgerald

1986 J. Nystrom & M. Wilander
G. Donnelly & P. Fleming

1987 K. Flach & R. Seguso
S. Casal & E. Sanchez

1988 K. Flach & R. Seguso
J. B. Fitzgerald & A. Jarryd

1989 J. B. Fitzgerald & A. Jarryd
R. Leach & J. Pugh

1990 R. Leach & J. Pugh
P. Aldrich & D. T. Visser

1991 J. B. Fitzgerald & A. Jarryd
J. Frana & L. Lavalle

1992 J. P. McEnroe & M. Stich
J. Grabb & R. A. Reneberg

1993 T. A. Woodbridge & M. Woodforde
G. Connell & P. Galbraith

1994 T. A. Woodbridge & M. Woodforde
G. Connell & P. Galbraith

1995 T. A. Woodbridge & M. Woodforde
R. Leach & S. Melville

1996 T. A. Woodbridge & M. Woodforde
B. Black & G. Connell

1997 T. A. Woodbridge & M. Woodforde
J. Eltingh & P. Haarhuis

1998 J. Eltingh & P. Haarhuis
T. A. Woodbridge & M. Woodforde

1999 M. Bhupathi & L. Paes
P. Haarhuis & J. Palmer

2000 T. A. Woodbridge & M. Woodforde
P. Haarhuis & S. Stolle

2001 D. Johnson & J. Palmer
J. Novak & D. Rikl

2002 J. Bjorkman & T. A Woodbridge
M. Knowles & D. Nestor

2003 J. Bjorkman & T. A Woodbridge
M. Bhupathi & M. Mirnyi

2004 J. Bjorkman & T. A Woodbridge
J. Knowle & N. Zimonjic

2005 S. Huss & W. Moodie
B. Bryan & M. Bryan

2006 B. Bryan & M. Bryan
F. Santoro & N. Zimonjic

LADIES' DOUBLES—CHAMPIONS & RUNNERS UP

1913 Mrs. R. J. McNair & Miss D. P. Boothby
Mrs. A. Sterry & Mrs. Lambert Chambers

1914 Miss E. Ryan & Miss A. M. Morton
Mrs. D. R. Larcombe & Mrs. F. J. Hannam

1919 Mlle. S. Lenglen & Miss E. Ryan
Mrs. Lambert Chambers & Mrs. D. R. Larcombe

1920 Mlle. S. Lenglen & Miss E. Ryan
Mrs. Lambert Chambers & Mrs. D. R. Larcombe

1921 Mlle. S. Lenglen & Miss E. Ryan
Mrs. A. E. Beamish & Mrs. G. E. Peacock

1922 Mlle. S. Lenglen & Miss E. Ryan
Mrs. A. D. Stocks & Miss K. McKane

1923 Mlle. S. Lenglen & Miss E. Ryan
Miss J. Austin & Miss E. L. Colyer

1924 Mrs. H. Wightman & Miss H. Wills
Mrs. B. C. Covell & Miss K. McKane

1925 Mlle. S. Lenglen & Miss E. Ryan
Mrs. A. V. Bridge & Mrs. C. G. McIlquham

1926 Miss E. Ryan & Miss M. K. Browne
Mrs. L. A. Godfree & Miss E. L. Colyer

1927 Miss H. Wills & Miss E. Ryan
Miss E. L. Heine & Mrs. G. E. Peacock

1928 Mrs. Holcroft-Watson & Miss P. Saunders
Miss E. H. Harvey & Miss E. Bennett

1929 Mrs. Holcroft-Watson & Mrs. L.R.C. Michell
Mrs. B. C. Covell & Mrs. D. C. Shepherd-Barron

1930 Mrs. F. S. Moody & Miss E. Ryan
Miss E. Cross & Miss S. Palfrey

1931 Mrs.D.C. Shepherd-Barron & MissP.E. Mudford
Mlle. D. Metaxa & Mlle. J. Sigart

1932 Mlle. D. Metaxa & Mlle. J. Sigart
Miss E. Ryan & Miss H. H. Jacobs

1933 Mme. R. Mathieu & Miss E. Ryan
Miss F. James & Miss A. M. Yorke

1934 Mme. R. Mathieu & Miss E. Ryan
Mrs. D. Andrus & Mme. S. Henrotin

1935 Miss F. James & Miss K. E. Stammers
Mme. R. Mathieu & Frau. S. Sperling

1936 Miss F. James & Miss K. E. Stammers
Mrs. S. P. Fabyan & Miss H. H. Jacobs

1937 Mme. R. Mathieu & Miss A. M. Yorke
Mrs. M. R. King & Mrs. J. B. Pittman

1938 Mrs. S. P. Fabyan & Miss A. Marble
Mme. R. Mathieu & Miss A. M. Yorke

1939 Mrs S. P. Fabyan & Miss A. Marble
Miss H. H. Jacobs & Miss A. M. Yorke

1946 Miss L. Brough & Miss M. Osborne
Miss P. Betz & Miss D. Hart

1947 Miss D. Hart & Mrs. P. C. Todd
Miss L. Brough & Miss M. Osborne

1948 Miss L. Brough & Mrs. W. du Pont
Miss D. Hart & Mrs. P. C. Todd

1949 Miss L. Brough & Mrs. W. du Pont
Miss G. Moran & Mrs. P. C. Todd

1950 Miss L. Brough & Mrs. W. du Pont
Miss S. Fry & Miss D. Hart

1951 Miss S. Fry & Miss D. Hart
Miss L. Brough & Mrs. W. du Pont

1952 Miss S. Fry & Miss D. Hart
Miss L. Brough & Miss M. Connolly

1953 Miss S. Fry & Miss D. Hart
Miss M. Connolly & Miss J. Sampson

1954 Miss L. Brough & Mrs. W. du Pont
Miss S. Fry & Miss D. Hart

1955 Miss A. Mortimer & Miss J. A. Shilcock
Miss S. J. Bloomer & Miss P. E. Ward

1956 Miss A. Buxton & Miss A. Gibson
Miss F. Muller & Miss D. G. Seeney

1957 Miss A. Gibson & Miss D. R. Hard
Mrs. K. Hawton & Mrs. T. D. Long

1958 Miss M. E. Bueno & Miss A. Gibson
Mrs. W. du Pont & Miss M. Varner

1959 Miss J. Arth & Miss D. R. Hard
Mrs. J. G. Fleitz & Miss C. C. Truman

1960 Miss M. E. Bueno & Miss D. R. Hard
Miss S. Reynolds & Miss R. Schuurman

1961 Miss K. Hantze & Miss B. J. Moffitt
Miss J. Lehane & Miss M. Smith

1962 Miss B. J. Moffitt & Mrs. J. R. Susman
Mrs. L. E. G. Price & Miss R. Schuurman

1963 Miss M. E. Bueno & Miss D. R. Hard
Miss R. A. Ebbern & Miss M. Smith

1964 Miss M. Smith & Miss L. R. Turner
Miss B. J. Moffitt & Mrs. J. R. Susman

1965 Miss M. E. Bueno & Miss B. J. Moffitt
Miss F. Durr & Miss J. LieVrig

1966 Miss M. E. Bueno & Miss N. Richey
Miss M. Smith & Miss J. A. M. Tegart

1967 Miss R. Casals & Mrs. L. W. King
Miss M. E. Bueno & Miss N. Richey

1968 Miss R. Casals & Mrs. L. W. King
Miss F. Durr & Mrs. P. F. Jones

1969 Mrs. B. M. Court & Miss J. A. M. Tegart
Miss P. S. A. Hogan & Miss M. Michel

1970 Miss R. Casals & Mrs. L. W. King
Miss F. Durr & Miss S. V. Wade

1971 Miss R. Casals & Mrs. L. W. King
Mrs. B. M. Court & Miss E. F. Goolagong

1972 Mrs. L. W. King & Miss B. F. Stove
Mrs. D. E. Dalton & Miss F. Durr

1973 Miss R. Casals & Mrs. L. W. King
Miss F. Durr & Miss B. F. Stove

1974 Miss E. F. Goolagong & Miss M. Michel
Miss H. F. Gourlay & Miss K. M. Krantzcke

1975 Miss A. Kiyomura & Miss K. Sawamatsu
Miss F. Durr & Miss B. F. Stove

1976 Miss C. M. Evert & Miss M. Navratilova
Mrs. L. W. King & Miss B. F. Stove

1977 Mrs. H. F. Gourlay Cawley & Miss J. C. Russell
Miss M. Navratilova & Miss B. F . Stove

1978 Mrs. G. E. Reid & Miss. W. M. Turnbull
Miss M. Jausovec & Miss V. Ruzici

1979 Mrs. L. W. King & Miss M. Navratilova
Miss B. F. Stove & Miss W. M. Turnbull

1980 Miss K. Jordan & Miss A. E. Smith
Miss R. Casals & Miss W. M. Turnbull

1981 Miss M. Navratilova & Miss P. H. Shriver
Miss K. Jordan & Miss A. E. Smith

1982 Miss M. Navratilova & Miss P. H. Shriver
Miss K. Jordan & Miss A. E. Smith

1983 Miss M. Navratilova & Miss P. H. Shriver
Miss R. Casals & Miss W. M. Turnbull

1984 Miss M. Navratilova & Miss P. H. Shriver
Miss K. Jordan & Miss A. E. Smith

1985 Miss K. Jordan & Mrs. P. D. Smylie
Miss M. Navratilova & Miss P. H. Shriver

1986 Miss M. Navratilova & Miss P. H. Shriver
Miss H. Mandlikova & Miss W. M. Turnbull

1987 Miss C. Kohde-Kilsch & Miss H. Sukova
Miss B. Nagelsen & Mrs. P. D. Smylie

1988 Miss S. Graf & Miss G. Sabatini
Miss L. Savchenko & Miss N. Zvereva

1989 Miss J. Novotna & Miss H. Sukova
Miss L. Savchenko & Miss N. Zvereva

1990 Miss J. Novotna & Miss H. Sukova
Miss K. Jordan & Mrs. P. D. Smylie

1991 Miss L. Savchenko & Miss N. Zvereva
Miss G. Fernandez & Miss J. Novotna

1992 Miss G. Fernandez & Miss N. Zvereva
Miss J. Novotna & Mrs. L. Savchenko-Neiland

1993 Miss G. Fernandez & Miss N. Zvereva
Mrs. L. Neiland & Miss J. Novotna

1994 Miss G. Fernandez & Miss N. Zvereva
Miss J. Novotna & Miss A. Sanchez Vicario

1995 Miss J. Novotna & Miss A. Sanchez Vicario
Miss G. Fernandez & Miss N. Zvereva

1996 Miss M. Hingis & Miss H. Sukova
Miss M.J. McGrath & Mrs. L. Neiland

1997 Miss G. Fernandez & Miss N. Zvereva
Miss N.J. Arendt & Miss M.M. Bollegraf

1998 Miss M. Hingis & Miss J. Novotna
Miss L.A. Davenport & Miss N. Zvereva

1999 Miss L.A. Davenport & Miss C. Morariu
Miss M. de Swardt & Miss E. Tatarkova

2000 Miss S. Williams & Miss V. Williams
Mrs J. Halard–Decugis & Miss A. Sugiyama

2001 Miss L.M. Raymond & Miss R.P. Stubbs
Miss K. Clijsters & Miss A. Sugiyama

2002 Miss S. Williams & Miss V. Williams
Miss V. Ruano Pascual & Miss P. Suarez

2003 Miss K. Clijsters & Miss A. Sugiyama
Miss V. Ruano Pascual & Miss P. Suarez

2004 Miss C. Black & Miss R.P. Stubbs
Mrs L. Huber & Miss A. Sugiyama

2005 Miss C. Black & Mrs L. Huber
Miss S. Kuznetsova & Miss A. Muresmo

2005 Miss Z. Yan & Miss J. Zheng
Miss V. Ruano Pascual & Miss P. Suarez

THE CHAMPIONSHIP ROLL

MIXED DOUBLES—CHAMPIONS & RUNNERS UP

1913 H. Crisp and Mrs. C. O. Tuckey
J. C. Parke and Mrs. D. R. Larcombe

1914 J. C. Parke and Mrs. D.R. Larcombe
A. F. Wilding and Mlle. M. Broquedis

1919 R. Lycett and Miss E. Ryan
A. D. Prebble and Mrs. Lambert Chambers

1920 G. L. Patterson and Mlle. S. Lenglen
R. Lycett and Miss E. Ryan

1921 R. Lycett and Miss E. Ryan
M. Woosnam and Miss P. L. Howkins

1922 P. O'Hara-Wood and Mlle. S. Lenglen
R. Lycett and Miss E. Ryan

1923 R. Lycett and Miss E. Ryan
L. S. Deane and Mrs. D. C. Shepherd-Barron

1924 J. B. Gilbert and Miss K. McKane
L. A. Godfree and Mrs. D. C. Shepherd-Barron

1925 J. Borotra and Mlle. S. Lenglen
H. L. de Morpurgo and Miss E. Ryan

1926 L. A. Godfree and Mrs. L. A. Godfree
H. Kinsey and Miss M. K. Browne

1927 F. T. Hunter and Miss E. Ryan
L. A. Godfree and Mrs. L. A. Godfree

1928 P. D. B. Spence and Miss E. Ryan
J. Crawford and Miss D. Akhurst

1929 F. T. Hunter and Miss H. Wills
I. G. Collins and Miss J. Fry

1930 J. H. Crawford and Miss E. Ryan
D. Prenn and Fraulein H. Krahwinkel

1931 G. M. Lott and Mrs L. A. Harper
I. G. Collins and Miss J. C. Ridley

1932 E. Maier and Miss E. Ryan
H. C. Hopman and Mlle. J. Sigart

1933 G. von Cramm and Fraulein H. Krahwinkel
N. G. Farquharson and Miss M. Heeley

1934 R. Miki and Miss D. E. Round
H. W. Austin and Mrs D. C. Shepherd-Barron

1935 F. J. Perry and Miss D. E. Round
H. C. Hopman and Mrs. H. C. Hopman

1936 F. J. Perry and Miss D. E. Round
J. D. Budge and Mrs. S. P. Fabyan

1937 J. D. Budge and Miss A. Marble
Y. Petra and Mme. R. Mathieu

1938 J. D. Budge and Miss A. Marble
H. Henkel and Mrs. S. P. Fabyan

1939 R. L. Riggs and Miss A. Marble
F. H. D. Wilde and Miss N. B. Brown

1946 T. Brown and Miss L. Brough
G. E. Brown and Miss D. Bundy

1947 J. E. Bromwich and Miss L. Brough
C. F. Long and Mrs. N. M. Bolton

1948 J. E. Bromwich and Miss L. Brough
F. A. Sedgman and Miss D. Hart

1949 E. W. Sturgess and Mrs. S. P. Summers
J. E. Bromwich and Miss L. Brough

1950 E. W. Sturgess and Miss L. Brough
G. E. Brown and Mrs. P. C. Todd

1951 F. A. Sedgman and Miss D. Hart
M. G. Rose and Mrs. N. M. Bolton

1952 F. A. Sedgman and Miss D. Hart
E. Morea and Mrs. T. D. Long

1953 V. Seixas and Miss D. Hart
E. Morea and Miss S. Fry

1954 V. Seixas and Miss D. Hart
K. R. Rosewall and Mrs. W. du Pont

1955 V. Seixas and Miss D. Hart
E. Morea and Miss L. Brough

1956 V. Seixas and Miss S. Fry
G. Mulloy and Miss A. Gibson

1957 M. G. Rose and Miss D. R. Hard
N. A. Fraser and Miss A. Gibson

1958 R. N. Howe and Miss L. Coghlan
K. Nielsen and Miss A. Gibson

1959 R. Laver and Miss D. R. Hard
N. A. Fraser and Miss M. E. Bueno

1960 R. Laver and Miss D. R. Hard
R. N. Howe and Miss M. E. Bueno

1961 F. S. Stolle and Miss L. R. Turner
R. N. Howe and Miss E. Buding

1962 N. A. Fraser and Mrs. W. du Pont
R. D. Ralston and Miss A. S. Haydon

1963 K. N. Fletcher and Miss M. Smith
R. A. J. Hewitt and Miss D. R. Hard

1964 F. S. Stolle and Miss L. R. Turner
K. N. Fletcher and Miss M. Smith

1965 K. N. Fletcher and Miss M. Smith
A. D. Roche and Miss J. A. M. Tegart

1966 K. N. Fletcher and Miss M. Smith
R. D. Ralston amd Mrs. L. W. King

1967 O. K. Davidson and Mrs. L. W. King
K. N. Fletcher and Miss M. E. Bueno

1968 K. N. Fletcher and Mrs. B. M. Court
A. Metreveli and Miss O. Morozova

1969 F. S. Stolle and Mrs. P. F. Jones
A. D. Roche and Miss J. A. M. Tegart

1970 I. Nastase and Miss R. Casals
A. Metreveli and Miss O. Morozova

1971 O. K. Davidson and Mrs. L. W. King
M. C. Riessen and Mrs. B. M. Court

1972 I. Nastase and Miss R. Casals
K.G. Warwick and Miss E. F. Goolagong

1973 O. K. Davidson and Mrs. L. W. King
R. Ramirez and Miss J. S. Newberry

1974 O. K. Davidson and Mrs. L. W. King
M. J. Farrell and Miss L. J. Charles

1975 M. C. Riessen and Mrs. B. M. Court
A. J. Stone and Miss B. F. Stove

1976 A. D. Roche and Miss F. Durr
R. L. Stockton and Miss R. Casals

1977 R. A. J. Hewitt and Miss G. R. Stevens
F. D. McMillan and Miss B. F. Stove

1978 F. D. McMillan and Miss B. F. Stove
R. O. Ruffels and Mrs. L. W. King

1979 R. A. J. Hewitt and Miss G. R. Stevens
F. D. McMillan and Miss B. F. Stove

1980 J. R. Austin and Miss T. Austin
M. R. Edmondson and Miss D. L. Fromholtz

1981 F. D. McMillan and Miss B. F. Stove
J. R. Austin and Miss T. Austin

1982 K. Curren and Miss A. E. Smith
J. M. Lloyd and Miss W. M. Turnbull

1983 J. M. Lloyd and Miss W. M. Turnbull
S. Denton and Mrs. L. W. King

1984 J. M. Lloyd and Miss W. M. Turnbull
S. Denton and Miss K. Jordan

1985 P. McNamee and Miss M. Navratilova
J. B. Fitzgerald and Mrs. P. D. Smylie

1986 K. Flach and Miss K. Jordan
H. P. Guenthardt and Miss M. Navratilova

1987 M. J. Bates and Miss J. M. Durie
D. Cahill and Miss N. Provis

1988 S. E. Stewart and Miss Z. L. Garrison
K. Jones and Mrs. S. W. Magers

1989 J. Pugh and Miss J. Novotna
M. Kratzmann and Miss J. M. Byrne

1990 R. Leach and Miss Z. L. Garrison
J. B. Fitzgerald and Mrs P. D. Smylie

1991 J. B. Fitzgerald and Mrs. P. D. Smylie
J. Pugh and Miss N. Zvereva

1992 C. Suk and Mrs L. Savchenko-Neiland
J. Eltingh and Miss M. Oremans

1993 M. Woodforde and Miss M. Navratilova
T. Nijssen and Miss M. M. Bollegraf

1994 T. A. Woodbridge and Miss H. Sukova
T. J. Middleton and Miss L. M. McNeil

1995 J. Stark and Miss M. Navratilova
C. Suk and Miss G. Fernandez

1996 C. Suk and Miss H. Sukova
M. Woodforde and Mrs. L. Neiland

1997 C. Suk and Miss H. Sukova
A. Olhovskiy and Mrs L. Neiland

1998 M. Mirnyi and Miss S. Williams
M. Bhupathi and Miss M. Lucic

1999 L. Paes and Miss L.M. Raymond
J. Bjorkman and Miss A. Kournikova

2000 D. Johnson and Miss K. Po
L. Hewitt and Miss K. Clijsters

2001 L. Friedl and Miss D. Hantuchova
M. Bryan and Mrs L. Huber

2002 M. Bhupathi and Miss E. Likhovtseva
K. Ullyett and Miss D. Hantuchova

2003 L. Paes and Miss M. Navratilova
A. Ram and Miss A. Rodionova

2004 W. Black and Miss C. Black
T.A. Woodbridge and Miss A. Molik

2005 M. Bhupathi and Miss M. Pierce
P. Hanley and Miss T. Perebiynis

2006 A. Ram and Miss V. Zvonareva
B. Bryan and Miss V. Williams

BOYS' SINGLES

1947 K. Nielsen (Denmark) *S. V. Davidson (Sweden)*	1962 S. Matthews (G.B.) *A. Metreveli (U.S.S.R.)*	1977 V. A. Winitsky (U.S.A.) *T. E. Teltscher (U.S.A.)*	1992 D. Skoch (Czechoslovakia) *B. Dunn (U.S.A.)*
1948 S. Stockenberg (Sweden) *D. Vad (Hungary)*	1963 N. Kalogeropoulos (Greece) *I. El Shafei (U.A.R.)*	1978 I. Lendl (Czechoslovakia) *J. Turpin (U.S.A.)*	1993 R. Sabau (Romania) *J. Szymanski (Venezuela)*
1949 S. Stockenberg (Sweden) *J. A.T. Horn (G.B.)*	1964 I. El Shafei (U.A.R.) *V. Korotkov (U.S.S.R.)*	1979 R. Krishnan (India) *D. Siegler (U.S.A.)*	1994 S. Humphries (U.S.A.) *M. A. Philippoussis (Australia)*
1950 J. A.T. Horn (G.B.) *K. Mobarek (Egypt)*	1965 V. Korotkov (U.S.S.R.) *G. Goven (France)*	1980 T. Tulasne (France) *H. D. Beutel (Germany)*	1995 O. Mutis (France) *N. Kiefer (Germany)*
1951 J. Kupferburger (S.A.) *K. Mobarek (Egypt)*	1966 V. Korotkov (U.S.S.R.) *B. E. Fairlie (N.Z.)*	1981 M. W. Anger (U.S.A.) *P. Cash (Australia)*	1996 V. Voltchkov (Belarus) *I. Ljubicic (Croatia)*
1952 R. K. Wilson (G.B.) *T. T. Fancutt (S.A.)*	1967 M. Orantes (Spain) *M. S. Estep (U.S.A.)*	1982 P. Cash (Australia) *H. Sundstrom (Sweden)*	1997 W. Whitehouse (South Africa) *D. Elsner (Germany)*
1953 W. A. Knight (G.B.) *R. Krishnan (India)*	1968 J. G. Alexander (Australia) *J. Thamin (France)*	1983 S. Edberg (Sweden) *J. Frawley (Australia)*	1998 R. Federer (Switzerland) *I. Labadze (Georgia)*
1954 R. Krishnan (India) *A. J. Cooper (Australia)*	1969 B. Bertram (S.A.) *J. G. Alexander (Australia)*	1984 M.Kratzmann (Australia) *S. Kruger (S.A.)*	1999 J. Melzer (Austria) *K. Pless (Denmark)*
1955 M. P. Hann (G.B.) *J. E. Lundquist (Sweden)*	1970 B. Bertram (S.A.) *F. Gebert (Germany)*	1985 L. Lavalle (Mexico) *E. Velez (Mexico)*	2000 N. Mahut (France) *M. Ancic (Croatia)*
1956 R. Holmberg (U.S.A.) *R. G. Laver (Australia)*	1971 R. Kreiss (U.S.A.) *S. A. Warboys (G.B.)*	1986 E. Velez (Mexico) *J. Sanchez (Spain)*	2001 R. Valent (Switzerland) *G. Muller (Luxembourg)*
1957 J. I. Tattersall (G.B.) *I. Ribeiro (Brazil)*	1972 B. Borg (Sweden) *C. J. Mottram (G.B.)*	1987 D. Nargiso (Italy) *J. R. Stoltenberg (Australia)*	2002 T. Reid (Australia) *L. Quahab (Algeria)*
1958 E. Buchholz (U.S.A.) *P. J. Lall (India)*	1973 W. Martin (U.S.A.) *C. S. Dowdeswell (Rhodesia)*	1988 N. Pereira (Venezuela) *G. Raoux (France)*	2003 F. Mergea (Romania) *C. Guccione (Australia)*
1959 T. Lejus (U.S.S.R.) *R. W. Barnes (Brazil)*	1974 W. Martin (U.S.A.) *Ash Amritraj (India)*	1989 N. Kulti (Sweden) *T. A. Woodbridge (Australia)*	2004 G. Monfils (France) *M. Kasiri (G.B.)*
1960 A. R. Mandelstam (S.A.) *J. Mukerjea (India)*	1975 C. J. Lewis (N.Z.) *R. Ycaza (Ecuador)*	1990 L. Paes (India) *M. Ondruska (S.A.)*	2005 J. Chardy (France) *R. Haase (Netherlands)*
1961 C. E. Graebner (U.S.A.) *E. Blanke (Austria)*	1976 H. Guenthardt (Switzerland) *P. Elter (Germany)*	1991 T. Enquist (Sweden) *M. Joyce (U.S.A.)*	2006 T. De Bakker (Netherlands) *M. Gawron (Poland)*

BOYS' DOUBLES

1982 P. Cash & J. Frawley *R. D. Leach & J. J. Ross*	1988 J. Stoltenberg & T. Woodbridge *D. Rikl & T. Zdrazila*	1994 B. Ellwood & M. Philippoussis *V. Platenik & R. Schlachter*	2001 F. Dancevic & G. Lapentti *B. Echagaray & S. Gonzales*
1983 M. Kratzmann & S. Youl *M. Nastase & O. Rahnasto*	1989 M. Lee & J. M. Stark *J-L. De Jager & W. R. Ferreira*	1995 M. Lee & J. M. Trotman *A. Hernandez & M. Puerta*	2002 F. Mergea & H. Tecau *B. Baker & B. Ram*
1984 R. Brown & R. Weiss *M. Kratzmann & J. Svensson*	1990 S. Lareau & S. Leblanc *C. Marsh & M. Ondruska*	1996 D. Bracciali & J. Robichaud *D. Roberts & W. Whitehouse*	2003 F. Mergea & H. Tecau *A. Feeney & C. Guccione*
1985 A. Moreno & J. Yzaga *P. Korda & C. Suk*	1991 K. Alami & G. Rusedski *J-L. De Jager & A. Medvedev*	1997 L. Horna & N. Massu *J. Van de Westhuizen & W. Whitehouse*	2004 B. Evans & S. Oudsema *R. Haase & V. Troicki*
1986 T. Carbonell & P. Korda *S. Barr & H. Karrasch*	1992 S. Baldas & S. Draper *M. S. Bhupathi & N. Kirtane*	1998 R. Federer & O. Rochus *M. Llodra & A. Ram*	2005 J. Levine & M. Shabaz *S. Groth & A. Kennaugh*
1987 J. Stoltenberg & T. Woodbridge *D. Nargiso & E. Rossi*	1993 S. Downs & J. Greenhalgh *N. Godwin & G. Williams*	1999 G. Coria & D. Nalbandian *T. Enev & J. Nieminem*	2006 K. Damico & N. Schnugg *M. Klizan & A. Martin*
		2000 D. Coene & K. Vliegen *A. Banks & B. Riby*	

GIRLS' SINGLES

1947 Miss G. Domken (Belgium) *Miss B. Wallen (Sweden)*	1962 Miss G. Baksheeva (U.S.S.R.) *Miss E. P. Terry (N.Z.)*	1977 Miss L. Antonoplis (U.S.A) *Miss Mareen Louie (U.S.A.)*	1992 Miss C. Rubin (U.S.A) *Miss L. Courtois (Belgium)*
1948 Miss O. Miskova (Czechoslovakia) *Miss V. Rigollet (Switzerland)*	1963 Miss D. M. Salfati (France) *Miss K. Dening (Australia)*	1978 Miss T. Austin (U.S.A) *Miss H. Mandlikova (Czechoslovakia)*	1993 Miss N. Feber (Belgium) *Miss R. Grande (Italy)*
1949 Miss C. Mercelis (Belgium) *Miss J. S. V. Partridge (G.B.)*	1964 Miss P. Bartkowicz (U.S.A) *Miss E. Subirats (Mexico)*	1979 Miss M. L. Piatek (U.S.A) *Miss A. A. Moulton (U.S.A.)*	1994 Miss M. Hingis (Switzerland) *Miss M-R. Jeon (Korea)*
1950 Miss L. Cornell (G.B.) *Miss A. Winter (Norway)*	1965 Miss O. Morozova (U.S.S.R.) *Miss R. Giscarfe (Argentina)*	1980 Miss D. Freeman (Australia) *Miss S. J. Leo (Australia)*	1995 Miss A. Olsza (Poland) *Miss T. Tanasugarn (Thailand)*
1951 Miss L. Cornell (G.B.) *Miss C. Lazzarino (Italy)*	1966 Miss B. Lindstrom (Finland) *Miss J. A. Congdon (g.b)*	1981 Miss Z. Garrison (U.S.A) *Miss R. R. Uys (S.A.)*	1996 Miss A. Mauresmo (France) *Miss M. L. Serna (Spain)*
1952 Miss F. J. I. ten Bosch (Netherlands) *Miss R. Davar (India)*	1967 Miss J. Salome (Netherlands) *Miss E. M. Strandberg (Sweden)*	1982 Miss C. Tanvier (France) *Miss H. Sukova (Czechoslovakia)*	1997 Miss C. Black (Zimbabwe) *Miss A. Rippner (U.S.A.)*
1953 Miss D. Kilian (S.A.) *Miss V. A. Pitt (G.B.)*	1968 Miss K. Pigeon (U.S.A) *Miss L. E. Hunt (Australia)*	1983 Miss P. Paradis (France) *Miss P. Hy (Hong Kong)*	1998 Miss K. Srebotnik (Slovenia) *Miss K. Clijsters (Belgium)*
1954 Miss V. A. Pitt (G.B.) *Miss C. Monnot (France)*	1969 Miss K. Sawamatsu (Japan) *Miss B. I. Kirk (S.A.)*	1984 Miss A. N. Croft (G.B.) *Miss E. Reinach (S.A.)*	1999 Miss I. Tulyagnova (Uzbekhistan) *Miss L. Krasnoroutskaya (U.S.S.R.)*
1955 Miss S. M. Armstrong (G.B.) *Miss B. de Chambure (France)*	1970 Miss S. Walsh (U.S.A) *Miss M. V. Kroshina (U.S.S.R.)*	1985 Miss A. Holikova (Czechoslovakia) *Miss J. M. Byrne (Australia)*	2000 Miss M. E. Salerni (Argentina) *Miss T. Perebiynis (Ukraine)*
1956 Miss A. S. Haydon (G.B.) *Miss I. Buding (Germany)*	1971 Miss M.V. Kroschina (U.S.S.R.) *Miss S. H. Minford (G.B.)*	1986 Miss N.M. Zvereva (U.S.S.R.) *Miss L. Meskhi (U.S.S.R.)*	2001 Miss A. Widjaja (Indonesia) *Miss D. Safina (U.S.S.R.)*
1957 Miss M. Arnold (U.S.A.) *Miss E. Reyes (Mexico)*	1972 Miss I. Kloss (S.A.) *Miss G. L. Coles (g.b)*	1987 Miss N.M. Zvereva (U.S.S.R.) *Miss J. Halard (France)*	2002 Miss V. Douchevina (Russia) *Miss M. Sharapova (U.S.S.R.)*
1958 Miss S. M. Moore (U.S.A.) *Miss A. Dmitrieva (U.S.S.R.)*	1973 Miss A. Kiyomura (U.S.A.) *Miss M. Navratilova (Czechoslovakia)*	1988 Miss B. Schultz (Netherlands) *Miss E. Derly (France)*	2003 Miss K. Flipkens (Belgium) *Miss A. Tchakvetadze (U.S.S.R.)*
1959 Miss J. Cross (S.A.) *Miss D. Schuster (Austria)*	1974 Miss M. Jausovec (Yugoslavia) *Miss M. Simionescu (Romania)*	1989 Miss A. Strnadova (Czechoslovakia) *Miss M. J. McGrath (U.S.A.)*	2004 Miss K. Bondarenko (Ukraine) *Miss A. Ivanovic (Serbia and Montenegro)*
1960 Miss K. Hantze (U.S.A) *Miss L. M Hutchings (S.A.)*	1975 Miss N. Y. Chmyreva (U.S.S.R.) *Miss R. Marsikova (Czechoslovakia)*	1990 Miss A. Strnadova (Czechoslovakia) *Miss K. Sharpe (Australia)*	2005 Miss A. Radwanska (Poland) *Miss T. Paszek (Austria)*
1961 Miss G. Baksheeva (U.S.S.R.) *Miss K. D. Chabot (U.S.A.)*	1976 Miss N. Y. Chmyreva (U.S.S.R.) *Miss M. Kruger (S.A.)*	1991 Miss B. Rittner (Germany) *Miss E. Makarova (U.S.S.R.)*	2006 Miss C. Wozniacki (Denmark) *Miss M. Rybarikova (Slovakia)*

GIRLS' DOUBLES

1982 Miss B. Herr & Miss P. Barg *Miss B. S. Gerken & Miss G. A. Rush*	1988 Miss J. A. Faull & Miss R. McQuillan *Miss A. Dechaume & Miss E. Derly*	1995 Miss C. Black & Miss A. Olsza *Miss T. Musgrove & Miss J Richardson*	2001 Miss G. Dulko & Miss A. Harkleroad *Miss C. Horiatopoulos & Miss B. Mattek*
1983 Miss P. Fendick & Miss P. Hy *Miss C. Anderholm & Miss H. Olsson*	1989 Miss J. Capriati & Miss M. McGrath *Miss A. Strnadova & Miss E. Sviglerova*	1996 Miss O. Barabanschikova & Miss A. Mauresmo *Miss L. Osterloh & Miss S. Reeves*	2002 Miss E. Clijsters & Miss B. Strycova *Miss A. Baker & Miss A-L. Groenfeld*
1984 Miss C. Kuhlman & Miss S. Rehe *Miss V. Milvidskaya & Miss L.I. Savchenko*	1990 Miss K. Habsudova & Miss A. Strnadova *Miss N. J. Pratt & Miss K. Sharpe*	1997 Miss C. Black & Miss I. Selyutina *Miss M. Matevzic & Miss K. Srebotnik*	2003 Miss A. Kleybanova & Miss S. Mirza *Miss K. Bohmova & Miss M. Krajicek*
1985 Miss L. Field & Miss J. Thompson *Miss E. Reinach & Miss J. A. Richardson*	1991 Miss C. Barclay & Miss L. Zaltz *Miss J. Limmer & Miss A. Woolcock*	1998 Miss E. Dyrberg & Miss J. Kostanic *Miss P. Rampre & Miss I. Tulyaganova*	2004 Miss V. Azarenka & Miss V. Havartsova *Miss M. Erakovic & Miss M. Niculescu*
1986 Miss M. Jaggard & Miss L. O'Neill *Miss L. Meskhi & Miss N. M. Zvereva*	1992 Miss M. Avotins & Miss L. McShea *Miss P. Nelson & Miss J. Steven*	1999 Miss D. Bedanova & Miss M.E. Salerni *Miss T. Perebiynis & Miss I. Tulyaganova*	2005 Miss V. Azarenka & Miss A. Szavay *Miss M. Erakovic & Miss M. Niculescu*
1987 Miss N. Medvedeva & Miss N.M. Zvereva *Miss I. S. Kim & Miss P. M. Moreno*	1993 Miss L. Courtois & Miss N. Feber *Miss H. Mochizuki & Miss Y. Yoshida*	2000 Miss I. Gaspar & Miss T. Perebiynis *Miss D. Bedanova & Miss M. E. Salerni*	2006 Miss A. Kleybanova & Miss A. Pavlyuchenkova *Miss A. Antoniychuk & Miss A. Dulgheru*
	1994 Miss E. De Villiers & Miss E. E. Jelfs *Miss C. M. Morariu & Miss L. Varmuzova*